First Church of Christ

An historical review. One hundred and fiftieth anniversary of the First Church of Christ in Amherst, Massachusetts.

November 7, 1889

First Church of Christ

An historical review. One hundred and fiftieth anniversary of the First Church of Christ in Amherst, Massachusetts. November 7, 1889

ISBN/EAN: 9783337260989

Printed in Europe, USA, Canada, Australia, Japan

Cover: Foto ©Lupo / pixelio.de

More available books at **www.hansebooks.com**

Church and Manse. Built 1867.

AN HISTORICAL REVIEW.

ONE HUNDRED AND FIFTIETH ANNIVERSARY

—— OF THE ——

FIRST CHURCH OF CHRIST

—— IN ——

AMHERST, MASSACHUSETTS.

NOVEMBER 7, 1889.

AMHERST, MASS.:
PRESS OF THE AMHERST RECORD.
1890.

CONTENTS.

	PAGE.
Preface,	5
Historical Address by Rev. G. S. Dickerman,	9
Presentation of Portraits by John H. Washburn and their Acceptance by Rev. D. W. Marsh, D. D.,	34
Address. The First and Second Pastors, by Rev. Chas. H. Williams.	36
Address. The Relation of the Church to the Educational Institutions of Amherst, by Prof. Wm. S. Tyler, D. D., LL.D.,	43
Address. Representative Men of the Parish, Church Buildings and Finances, by W. A. Dickinson.	50
Address. The Material Progress of Amherst, by Henry F. Hills,	67
Reminiscences of Former Pastors:	
Paper by Rev. Aaron M. Colton,	71
Paper by Rev. E. S. Dwight, D. D.,	78
Letter by Rev. Henry L. Hubbell, D. D.,	83
Address by Rev. Jonathan L. Jenkins, D. D..	86
Letter by Rev. F. F. Emerson,	88
Address by Rev. E. P. Blodgett,	91
Correspondence,	94
Hymn, by Dr. V. W. Leach,	99
Old Documents,	100
Appendix to Historical Address:	
A. Ancestry and Families of the Founders,	103
B. Petition against Building Two Meeting Houses,	112
C. Origin of the Second Church and Parish.	117
Statistical Tables,	122

ILLUSTRATIONS.

	PAGE.
Church and Manse,	Frontispiece
Portrait of Dr. Parsons,	34
Portrait of Mrs. Parsons,	35
Second Meeting House and Old Parsons House,	53
Third Meeting House,	57

PREFACE.

At a meeting of the Parish connected with the First Church of Amherst, February 11, 1889, the Pastor, Rev. G. S. Dickerman, made an informal presentation of the subject of commemorating in a suitable manner the Origin of the Church at the approaching One Hundred and Fiftieth Anniversary. It was thereupon voted to make suitable arrangements for the Celebration and Messrs. L. D. Hills, George Cutler and H. D. Fearing were appointed to nominate such Committees as they should think advisable and report at the Annual Meeting of the Parish in March.

At a meeting of the Church, similar action was taken and a Committee was appointed and authorized to cooperate with that of the Parish. By them committees were nominated, and these were chosen at the Parish Meeting, March 12, 1889, and were accepted by the Church. After certain modifications they stood as follows:

Historic Research.
REV. G. S. DICKERMAN,
OLIVER D. HUNT,
JAMES I. COOPER,

Entertainment.
P. E. IRISH,
J. A. RAWSON,
E. D. MARSH.

Invitations.
GEORGE MONTAGUE,
HENRY F. HILLS,
WM. W. HUNT,

Decorations.
MORRIS KINGMAN,
MISS FANNIE P. CUTLER,
MISS CARRIE T. HUNT.

Anniversary Exercises.
REV. G. S DICKERMAN,
FLAVEL GAYLORD,
WOLCOTT HAMLIN,

Portraits and Antiques.
REV. D. W. MARSH,
GEORGE GRAVES.

These Committees subsequently met for joint action, appointed additional Committees as seemed advisable and made the necessary preparation for the celebration.

ORDER OF EXERCISES.

THURSDAY MORNING, 9-30 O'CLOCK.

1. Organ Prelude.
2. Anthem.
3. Reading of Scriptures, Psalm CXXII.
4. Hymn. Tune "Dundee."

> "Let children hear the mighty deeds,
> Which God performed of old;
> Which in our younger years we saw,
> And which our fathers told.
>
> Our lips shall tell them to our sons,
> And they again to theirs,
> That generations yet unborn
> May teach them to their heirs."

5. Reading of the Ancient Covenant of the Church,
6. Lord's Supper.
   Rev. Rowland Ayres, D. D., Rev. Chas. H. Williams.
7. Hymn 820. "Let Saints below in concert sing."
8. Historical Address, - - Rev. G. S. Dickerman.
9. Hymn 329. "Coronation."
10. The First and Second Pastors, Rev. Chas. H. Williams.
11. Hymn 1060. "O God, beneath thy guiding hand."

Benediction.

Collation.

THURSDAY AFTERNOON, 1-30 O'CLOCK.

1. Organ Prelude.
2. Te Deum.
3. Prayer. Rev. J. L. Jenkins, D. D.
4. Response.
5. The Relations of the Church to the Educational Institutions of Amherst, Prof. Wm. S. Tyler, D. D., LL. D.
6. Hymn. Composed by Dr. V. W. Leach.

7. REPRESENTATIVE MEN OF THE PARISH, CHURCH BUILDINGS AND FINANCE, - - - *Wm. A. Dickinson, Esq.*
8. REMINISCENCES,
   Rev. Aaron M. Colton. Rev. E. S. Dwight, D. D.
9. THE MATERIAL PROGRESS OF AMHERST, *Mr. Henry F. Hills.*
10. HYMN 757. "Oh, where are kings and empires now."

BENEDICTION.

THURSDAY EVENING, 7 O'CLOCK.

1. ORGAN PRELUDE.
2. ANTHEM.
3. ADDRESS, *Rev. J. L. Jenkins, D. D.*
4. READING OF LETTERS FROM *Rev. F. F. Emerson and Others.*
5. ADDRESS, *Rev. E. P. Blodgett.*
6. PRAYER, *Rev. Chas. S. Nash.*
7. HYMN 1014. "Christ is coming! Let creation ——"

BENEDICTION.

The following is from an account of the Anniversary in the *Hampshire Gazette* of November 12, 1889:

"The day was bright and sunny, an ideal Indian summer day, and the occasion brought together a large number from the four villages of Amherst, and from Hadley and other towns around. In the audience were seen many aged people, some of whom could cover with their memory half the space of time under review.

At the close of the historical address a pleasant surprise occurred, Mr. John H. Washburn of New York, a son of Rev. Royal Washburn a former pastor, and a descendant, through his mother, of the first and second pastors, was introduced, and in graceful words presented to the church the framed portraits of his grandfather and grandmother Rev. Dr. David Parsons and wife. Rev. Dr. Marsh of Amherst accepted the portraits on behalf of the church.

At noon by the blowing of the self-same conch-shell that used to summon the people to church, the assembly was called to dinner, prepared by the ladies in the hall below. The Divine Blessing was invoked by Rev. Dr. J. M. Greene of Lowell. After which more than three hundred people were sumptuously feasted with good things.

At the evening exercises a crowded audience assembled, the calm, moonlight evening being favorable for both driving and walking. After the opening anthem, finely sung by the choir, Rev. Dr. Jenkins, pastor of the church from '66 to '76, spoke in his usual bright and interesting manner, giving recollections of his pastorate, closing with a panegyric on the church, the church of New England, as being the conservator of all that is best and noblest in the state—a field of action for the best talent and executive ability of all.

Letters of regret were read from many who were invited to be present, among them J. H. Sweetser of New York, Mrs. Electa S. Boltwood of Kansas, Rev. Dr. G. L. Walker of Hartford, Rev. O. R. Kingsbury, Dr. J. C. Greenough and Mrs. Greenough of Westfield. Dr. E. S. Dwight was unable to be present, but sent an excellent letter, which was read by Rev. Charles S. Nash. Rev. Forrest F. Emerson of Newport, pastor from '80 to '83, expected until the last moment to be present, but pastoral duties that he did not feel at liberty to put aside, prevented his coming. His paper was read by Rev. Dr. Marsh.

Quite a collection of old and modern portraits and photographs of pastors and prominent men and women of the church and town, were displayed in the lecture room of the church. Some interesting relics were also shown, such as ancient books, manuscript sermons of the older pastors, musical instruments used in the choir fifty years ago, the manacles used to confine the famous Stephen Burroughs, etc. Among the portraits were those of Rev. Daniel Clark, Dea. Eleazer Gaylord and wife, Pres. Hitchcock, Edward Dickinson, Leonard Hills, Dea. Ayres, S. C. Carter, Aaron Belden. There were excellent photographs of Rev. H. Kingsbury, Rev. Dr. Hubbell, Dea. Sweetser and wife, Dr. Gridley, Dr. Smith, Miss Esther Cutler and others.

A word of praise ought to be spoken in regard to the music interspersed throughout the exercises. Much time and thought had been spent upon the preparation of suitable pieces, and the choir and their leader Mrs. Sanderson, won well-deserved laurels in their execution, especially in the *Te Deum*, the *Dona Nobis*, and the time-honored " Strike the Cymbal." A quartette from the Agricultural College rendered the chant " Remember now thy Creator" in a most accurate and very impressive manner. The one hundred and fiftieth anniversary is over and now the church takes its strong and steadfast march along towards its two hundredth year."

HISTORICAL ADDRESS.

By G. S. DICKERMAN, Pastor.

Occasions similar to this on which we meet are growing familiar. A trait of our times is love of the retrospect with endeavor to reproduce the life of a former period.

The past interests us as showing the *fountain head* of streams that are flowing in the present; and often we are led to wonder at the depth and majesty of these streams as we trace them back to a quiet, secluded spring.

We are interested, too, in the *life* of the past. It is so unlike that of the present, not only in outward circumstances, but in many essential features, in modes of thinking, in ideas of duty, in the sentiment and practice which prevailed. This gives a peculiar zest to studies which might otherwise seem dull and covers them with an air almost of romance.

But such a review is more than entertaining; it can teach us much. There are lessons here to make us wise and strong, to raise our courage and kindle our ardor. For how can we call to mind the deeds of those who have gone before us and be unmoved? How can we reflect on their high purpose, their fidelity to conviction, their steadfast endurance in the way they believed to be right, with the far-reaching results that have ensued, and not be made truer and better for the work we have to perform?

In our old record book the first entry is, "Nov^{br} 1735, I Began my Ministry at Hadley." Then immediately below we read "Nov^{br} 7, 1739, David Parsons Jun. was ordained Pastor of the Chh of Christ in Hadley 3^{d} Precinct, which was gathered on that Day & consisted of the Persons hereafter mentioned:"

David Parsons, Pastor	John Cowls
Nath'l Kellogg	Aaron Smith
John Ingram	Ebenezer Kellogg
Sam'el Hawley	Jonathan Smith
Eleazer Mattun	Nath'el Smith
John Nash	Joseph Clary
Pelatiah Smith	Jonathan Cowls &
Ebenezer Dickinson	Richard Chauncey."

Here are the names of sixteen men. The youngest of these was the pastor whose age was twenty-seven and who was as yet unmarried. The other fifteen were all householders and fathers of children, their ages ranging from thirty-four to seventy-eight.

The method of founding a church through a band of chosen men had prevailed from the beginning of the New England settlements. In earlier times the number had been fixed at seven and these were named *pillars* in allusion to the text of Proverbs, " Wisdom hath builded her house, she hath hewn out her seven pillars." So the churches at New Haven, Northampton and Westfield were organized and probably most of those belonging to that period, though in many cases no record is left of the event. But the usage with respect to number was gradually modified to suit the exigency, and in the organization of this church the founders seem to have included all the men, with a single exception, who intended to become members.

Having started in this manner, the next step was to receive into the body such other Christians as might be ready to join them. This was done on the first of January following, when twenty-eight persons " were added by recommendation from other churches."

One of these was David Smith, a man somewhat younger than any of the founders but the pastor, and perhaps unmarried though, he seems to have taken his wife not far from this time. These reasons may account for his not being among the founders.

Besides him were twenty-seven women, the mothers, wives and sisters of the men I have named. Among them were three recently bereaved widows whose names remind us of Zechariah Field, Samuel Boltwood and John Ingram Jr., who had come with their families to the settlement and had fallen thus early before the exposures incident to life in a new country.

Zechariah Field had been a leading man and among the foremost in the movement for a new precinct and the establishment of a church. His name headed the second petition to the General Court for this object, and when the petition was granted, the first meeting of the precinct was held at his house. Samuel Boltwood had also been prominent in the movement and was one of the earliest officers of the precinct, while young John Ingram was so related to a number of the families that his death, like that of the other two, must have caused universal mourning.

The elder John Ingram was the patriarch of the settlement, his age being seventy-eight, and, besides his son, he had four daughters who were wives of founders and themselves members of the church. His own wife was the sister of Ebenezer Dickinson, and the widow of his son was a daughter of Samuel Boltwood.

Another who was advanced in life was Nathaniel Kellogg, then in his seventieth year. His wife was the sister of Samuel and Solomon Boltwood. One of his sons had married Elizabeth Ingram and a daughter was the wife of Ebenezer Dickinson.

Of the children of Zechariah Field two were married to Samuel and Joseph Hawley, another to Moses Warner, and his son John to a daughter of Samuel Boltwood.

In this way all the families of the settlement were closely interrelated.*

In the list of Christian women there are six whose husbands were not in the church. Part of these afterwards had the joy of seeing their husbands take the covenant and enter into "full communion."

The whole number of families represented in the church by either husband or wife was twenty-four. There were several others in the settlement besides these—in all about thirty families.

A remarkably full record of these old families is to be found in Judd's History of Hadley to which I am greatly indebted for the statements I here present.

I have intimated that the church was composed of adult members. There were only three or four besides the pastor who were unmarried, and only two of these who could be called, according to our way of speaking, young people. These two were Elizabeth Smith and Ruth Boltwood, maidens of seventeen. But let no one suppose that there was a lack of the youthful element in this community or in the congregations that gathered here for worship. I find the number of sons and daughters in this group of families to have been over one hundred and ninety, or an average of six to each household. I do not mean by this that there were so many at the time the church was organized, or at any one time. Some died early, some were born at

---

*Appendix A.

a later date, while a number were grown to maturity. But leaving out these, a fine company remains of children and youth, not less than eighty or ninety as I count them, of all sizes from the babe in his cradle to youth and maidens whose lives were opening into manhood and womanhood. And these, we may be sure, played no small part in this new enterprise. Then as now parents were intent on the welfare of their children, and their first thought was of their religious training.

It is contained in the records that four days after the church was started, the pastor baptized Jonathan, the son of Jonathan and Sarah Cowls, and that in less than a month later, he baptized three more children presented by their parents. There is not a little meaning in this, and as you read on down the long list of five hundred and eighty-three baptisms, nearly all of children, in that one pastorate, and then continue with the still longer list of the second pastorate, the meaning becomes more impressive with every added name. During this eighty years ministry of father and son there were baptized upwards of fourteen hundred persons (1447), of whom not less than thirteen hundred were children upon whom their parents sought the blessings of the Abrahamic covenant.

This speaks volumes for the family life of the place. The family filled the people's minds. And the life of each home was the stronger and deeper for the whole community's being so much like a single family, so bound together in ties of kinship.

There were no foreigners here then, and there were few who had not been all their life in this particular society. We can hardly comprehend this at the present day, when our communities are full of strangers from various parts of the world: especially is it hard to understand of a frontier settlement gathered in the woods.

But let us go back a step. Ask whence these thirty families came. We find they were from old Hadley village and from Hatfield, and there they belonged to a society whose kinships and common interests were the same as we have seen here, only on a larger scale. Hadley and Hatfield were almost like one community, and they had kept on their way together from the time of their common origin eighty years before.

They had been planted as follows. The colony of Hartford, which Thomas Hooker had founded with the company he led through the wilderness from Dorchester, was in discord. Their great leader had died, and the church to which he had ministered was rent into two factions headed on the one side by the "teaching elder," Rev. Samuel Stone, and on the other by the "ruling elder," William Goodwin. A detailed account of this quarrel is given by Dr. Walker in his *History of the First Church in Hartford*. I need only say that the strife was intensely bitter, and continued for some five or six years. The most strenuous efforts for reconciliation were made by the neighboring churches, and by those more distant in the colonies of New Haven and Massachusetts; but they failed to heal the schism. William Goodwin and those attached to his party undertook to withdraw and unite with the church in Wethersfield. This was not sanctioned by the council called in the case. Nor did any measures avail, till it was finally decided that the minority should leave Hartford and establish a new settlement.

It was this minority which removed to our immediate neighborhood and founded the settlement of Hadley and Hatfield. They built on both sides of the river, as had been done in Hartford, and hence in time became two communities.

This immigration took place in 1659, and with it the settlement began. It was not, however, a wholly unanticipated event. Six years before, a number of men from Windsor, Hartford and Springfield petitioned the General Court to grant them a plantation at Nonotuck,—the Indian name for the Connecticut Valley north and west of the mountains. Following this was a purchase of the land from the Indians and the location of two prospective plantations, one on either side of the river. Then came the settlement of Northampton by colonists from Springfield and Windsor in 1654. But there was a pause in the movement from Hartford till the schism in the church precipitated it and made it much more extensive than it would otherwise have been. Hence, if there was at the end impulse and swift action, it was only after years of careful planning.

Notice further, that Wethersfield was identified with Hartford, and that Windsor naturally joined in the emigration. The Goodwin faction had found sympathy in the Wethersfield church and recruits were easily enlisted there. Also the journey to the new country lay through Windsor and a number from that place were ready to join the company.

It would seem that the new colony in separating from the one at Hartford did not become estranged from the parent. Rather the bitterness of the old strife ceased from this hour. The settlers had gone into a new wilderness to meet hardships, to brave dangers, and some of them to die by the hand of the savage. How could any feelings be cherished but those of kindness and mutual interest! So it came to pass that relations of peculiar intimacy were sustained between the Connecticut towns and the dwellers in Hadley and Hatfield. Old acquaintanceships were continued. Social and business interchanges were as frequent as circumstance would allow. The men of the two regions served together in the Indian wars and their wives bore in mutual sympathy their sorrows and their joys. Brothers and sisters and cousins visited from one place to the other, and marriages back and forth were continually adding new family ties to those already existing. It was only four years after the emigration that the Rev. Samuel Stone's daughter, Rebekah, came with her husband, Timothy Nash, to join the Hadley colony. And it may be proper, in this connection, to note that among the original members of our church there sat side by side one who was a descendant of Rev. Samuel Stone (John Nash) and two others who were descended from Elder William Goodwin (David Smith and Mrs. Sarah Cowls).

The close connection with these Connecticut towns continued long. David Smith, that member of this church who was married near the time of the organization, went to Wethersfield for his wife. A few months later the pastor also went to Wethersfield and brought thence Eunice Wells to be the joy of his house. And in due time his son, the second pastor, betook himself also to Wethersfield and brought thence another rare jewel in the person of Harriet Williams.

And let me call your attention to a few facts that come out in an examination of those earliest families of Amherst. It is possible to trace most of their lines of descent back to the first settlements in New England. Thus we find that every one of the original members of this church was descended from some progenitor who came from Hartford or the adjoining towns.* We find, moreover, that the admixture with families from elsewhere is very small. We should surely suppose that Springfield families would have become greatly mingled with them, especially as that Springfield colony at Northampton was so near a neighbor. But it was otherwise. Of those first colonists from whom these founders sprung, three out of every four, or more than forty in all, whose names are known, were of these Connecticut towns. A few were of Springfield, while the rest were of New Haven, Stratford and five or six towns of Massachusetts Bay, with only one or two to each place. This shows that, with rare exceptions, the marriages during that whole period had kept within

*Appendix A.

the circle of the families that were neighbors before the exodus to Hadley. And these families, we know were of those immigrants who came from England to Massachusetts at the first settlement of the country. The Hartford church was organized at Newtown, now Cambridge, Mass., in or probably before 1633 and removed in 1636 to their permanent settlement. The Windsor church was organized at Plymouth, England, in 1629 and came thence in a body to Dorchester where they remained till about the time of the immigration to Hartford, when they also removed. The Wethersfield church was organized at Watertown a few months later than the Windsor church and took the line of march through the wilderness in the same year. These three churches contributed in nearly equal proportions the elements of which the Amherst community was composed, though the larger part was from Hartford.

It was just about a hundred years after those immigrations from the vicinity of Boston to the Connecticut Valley, that this settlement was begun. What a centennial our founders might have celebrated at that very hour, if it had been the custom to indulge in such festivities!

That had been an eventful century. But looking back upon it from the point of view at which we stand it seems like one of slow progress. The settlers in this region had been confronted from the beginning with one ever present danger, and a danger which remained for a score of years after this church was founded. When those families set out from Hartford for these Hadley meadows they little thought what a terror was to hang over their homes from the Indians, or how many lives were to be sacrificed in wars and massacres. This terror kept back the growth of the settlements. It made the people gather closely together in villages and forbade their reaching out, as in other parts of New England, to build their scattered farm-houses and occupy the country. So, after fifty years, the only towns in all this part of the state besides Hadley and Hatfield, were Springfield, Westfield, Northampton and Deerfield, and the only churches were the six belonging to these towns.

And in the later period of the settlement of this place, we find that the advance had quickened but little. There were small frontier communities at Sunderland, Northfield, Belchertown, South Hadley and Blandford, but these were only in their beginnings and were looked upon as doubtful experiments. Western Massachusetts, with the exception of the Connecticut valley and Westfield, was still a "great and terrible wilderness."

One of our elderly people tells me it is a tradition in her family that when the early settlers came from Hadley to this region of the Third Precinct their friends thought they should never see them again. They expected nothing better than that they would fall by the Indian's hatchet, or be lost in the swamps and forests. So keen was their dread of any remoteness from the village centers.

Yet notwithstanding the long delay in occupying the land what a story was that of the hundred years then closing! We can imagine the kind of tales that were told about the hearth-stone in those first log cabins of this settlement. Books were rare then and other sources of entertainment familiar to us were unknown. We may therefore, suppose that reminiscences engaged their leisure hours to an extent that is now unusual. Fathers and mothers kept in vivid remembrance the scenes in which they had borne a part and told them often to their children and grandchildren, who in turn rehearsed them to another generation. Doubtless in all these homes there was narrated many a story of family experiences that spanned the whole century and carried the listening group back along the family pilgrimage to the voyage across the Atlantic and even beyond, to ancestral homes in England.

Suppose ourselves, for example, in the cabin of Dr. Nathaniel Smith which stood where the house of Mr. John White now is, just over College Hill. We will choose an evening when Mrs. Smith's parents are there, the aged John Ingram and his wife Mehitable Dickinson. In the family are two small children Dorothy and Rebecca. All are grouped about the fire-place with its blazing logs, in the manner of those old times, when the little girl at her grandfather's knee calls for a story. The patriarch's face lights up with an approving smile, and he asks what sort of a story it shall be. As children are apt to do in such a case, they ask for a tale of his childhood. And we can imagine the way the venerable man begins, reminding them that he was born only two years after the settlement of Hadley, that his father was then a young man under twenty years of age, and that his grandfather Gardner was but forty-six. And then he may have told how that grandfather had lived to be eighty-one years old and had often talked to him as he was now talking to them, telling about *his* early home in England and of the oppressions which led so many of the noblest spirits of the age to leave their native land to plant colonies in America, telling of the voyage across the Atlantic, too, and of the vicissitudes which followed in years full of thrilling events, till the new home was finally located in Hadley. What materials long since lost that settler of Amherst must have had at his command out of which to make a narrative of the beginnings of New England! And then of his own times! of King Philip's war, of the massacre at Bloody Brook, of the Indian attacks on Hadley and Hatfield and Deerfield! He himself could recall all these events and tell many tales of personal encounters with the Indians, and probably of hairbreadth escapes.

The grandmother, too, could add her incidents, recounting the stories in her own family of the journey through the wilderness to Wethersfield, and thence to Hadley. She could tell of the alarms in the village among the women and children, when the men had been away in the Indian wars.

And then the Doctor had his tales also to tell—among others of the strange sickness and death of his grandfather, the good Deacon Philip Smith who, according to Cotton Mather, was " murdered with an hideous witchcraft."

Reminiscences like these were the natural entertainment of family gatherings and of the leisure hour in all those homes.

And in some there were tales to tell of tragic events which had befallen the family itself. In the home of Samuel Hawley, a grandson kept in remembrance the heroic deeds of " the brave Capt. Marshall who fell in the Narragansett fight." In five or six other homes there were children and grandchildren of Sergeant Samuel Boltwood famous for his bravery and strength, and they could narrate with pride his exploits and how he was slain at Deerfield. And finally in the family of Zechariah Field, the son and daughters could tell of their great uncle Samuel and their uncle Ebenezer who had been slain, one at Hatfield and the other at Deerfield, by the same dreaded enemy out of the wilderness.

By such tales, looking back over the sufferings and courageous endurance of those who had gone before them, we may be sure, the founders of this church and of this community strengthened themselves for the work they had taken in hand. Behind them was a whole century of heroism, and with a like heroic spirit they were prepared to meet whatever duties might fall to their lot.

But, all unbeknown to them, a new era was opening, and a different field was to be offered in which to exercise their powers and employ the strength that had come to them from sires of so noble a mould. The Indians were to vanish. The wilderness was to be cultivated till it should blossom as the rose. A great people was speedily to be evolved out of materials then maturing but as yet uncrystalized. And then should come the problems of social organization and of the state that was to be—religious problems, political problems, educational problems, industrial problems, problems of all science and of all philosophy.

We can see now that the experiences of that first hundred years was a discipline singularly adapted to prepare the people of this valley, as of all the colonies on the Atlantic coast, for the great duties that were awaiting them.

Of the part performed by the children of these valley settlers little needs to be said. We have only to remember what Massachusetts has done for the nation and what this valley has done for Massachusetts to understand that their part has not been altogether unworthy of their fathers.

From this survey of movements and conditions anterior to the settlement of this place let us now pass to the circumstances immediately connected with the event we celebrate.

The period in which this church had its beginning is conspicuous in the ecclesiastical history of New England as the period of the *Great Awakening*. The first signs of this awakening were shown in the immediate vicinity of this place at Northampton. Jonathan Edwards had become greatly alarmed at the prevailing worldliness and disorderly condition of the churches and was moved to direct his powerful preaching to a thorough reformation. Results quickly appeared. In December, 1734, a number of persons in his congregation, as he says, " were to all appearance, savingly converted, and some of them wrought upon in a remarkable manner." Through the winter the movement deepened and became general throughout the parish. " An earnest concern about the great things of religion and the eternal world became universal in all parts of the town and among persons of all degrees and all ages. They were wont very often to meet together in private houses for religious purposes; and such meetings were wont greatly to be thronged. Souls did, as it were, come by flocks to Jesus Christ. From day to day, for many months together, might be seen evident instances of sinners brought out of darkness into marvellous light."

All this was wonderful, and it seemed the more wonderful because revivals had become unusual. A profound impression was produced on neighboring churches. " In March, 1735, the revival began to be general in South Hadley, and about the same time in Suffield. It next appeared in Sunderland, Deerfield and Hatfield; and afterward at West Springfield, Long Meadow and Enfield; and then in Hadley Old Town, and in Northfield."

It was in the fall of this year, 1735, that David Parsons began his ministry with the people of this Third Precinct of Hadley. What a time and what a place in which to begin!

Of the circumstances connecting this beginning with that great revival of religion we are not told in our annals. Yet who can doubt that there was a connection and one that was most vital?

This was four years previous to the organization of the church. Pass over these four years and we are on the eve of another great religious movement—so great and so wide reaching that the former one seems only like the introduction to this.

On the day our fathers gathered here, two hundred and fifty years ago, to enter into solemn covenant together before God and to establish this church, George Whitefield on board ship was approaching Philadelphia; and in less than a year from that time, in the following October, he was on his way from Boston " to visit Edwards and the scene of the revival in 1735." On this journey he preached at Leicester, Brookfield and Coldspring, or Belchertown, as the place is now called. For an account of his experience at the next stage I will read from his Journal of Friday, Oct. 17. " Set out as soon as it was light and reached *Hadley*, a place where a great work of God was begun some few years ago. But lately the people of God have complained of deadness and losing their first love. However, as soon as I mentioned what God had done for their souls formerly, it was like putting fire to tinder. The remembrance of it quickened them, and caused many to weep sorely."

The occasion thus described marked the commencement of a new revival which quickly overspread Northampton, Hatfield and the other valley towns, as it was already spreading in other parts of the state and of the country.

Of this refreshing the Amherst church enjoyed its share. This is shown in the fact that during the next year and a half thirty-five new members were added, all but one in the way of "admission to full communion," or as we now should say " on confession of their faith." These were chiefly of the families already mentioned, the sons and daughters of parents belonging to the church. Most of them were young, their ages ranging in general from fifteen to twenty-five.

Two or three, at least, were older than twenty-five and some may have been under fifteen. A most precious ingathering, therefore, and full of promise for the future!

But there were other results of this revival than the accession of these new members. It deeply affected the moral and spiritual life of the community. We have proof of this in a paper drawn up at the time and signed by thirty-six men and thirty-four women. From this let me read a few sentences to show its tenor.

"It has of late pleased a kind and merciful God in a very wonderful manner to pour out his Spirit upon this people in awakening, convincing and convicting influences upon sinners and in refreshing and comforting influences upon saints. To the end we may guard against falling into sin or neglecting those duties God has required of us, and may obtain the continuance and increase of so glorious a mercy as we have for some considerable time enjoyed, we, in a humble dependence upon divine power and grace for assistance and strength, do agree to the following Covenant. That we will devote ourselves in our several places and according to our several capacities to the great business of a religious life, and truly endeavor that we may answer the great end of our being in the world, the glory of God and the everlasting good of ourselves and others."

Following this, is a careful specification of Christian duties such as "a strict observance of the Lord's day," faithful care of the interests of others, avoidance of slander and meddlesome gossip, fidelity in the family and careful abstinence from all impure and unbecoming conduct.

It is a suggestive fact that in the list of seventy names subscribed to this covenant we miss those of many who were members of the church while we find some sixteen that are not on the church roll. It may not surprise us that some genuine Christians should have hesitated to put their signatures to so solemn a covenant, but it does seem strange that any who could sign this paper should have failed to take the further step of uniting with the Lord's people. None the less, however, does this paper testify to the extent and pervasive power of the revival.

We have evidence to the same effect, also, from another source. We know that there was a division of sentiment in the churches and among the theologians of the period about Whitefield and the religious movement attending his work. Out of this grew a long and heated controversy. Among the contributions to this discussion we find the following testimonial from pastors of this region:

"We whose names are subscribed to this would hereby declare to the glory of God's grace that we judge that there has been a happy revival of religion in the congregations that have been committed to our pastoral care, and that there are many in them that by abiding manifestations of a serious religious and humble spirit, and a conscientious care and watchfulness in their behavior toward God and man give all grounds of charity towards them as having been sincere in the profession they have made. - - - We think the effect has been such, and still continues to be such as leaves no room reasonably to doubt of God's having been wonderfully in the midst of us, and such as has laid us under great obligations forever to admire and extol the riches of his grace in doing such great things for us.

   Stephen Williams, pastor of a church in Springfield.
   Peter Raynolds, Enfield (Conn.).
   Jonathan Edwards, Northampton.
   Samuel Allis, Somers (Conn.).
   John Woodbridge, Second Church, Hadley.
   David Parsons, Jr., Third Church, Hadley.
   Edward Billings, Coldspring.
   Timothy Woodbridge, Hatfield.
   Chester Williams, First Church, Hadley."

We learn thus of the happy spiritual conditions which encompassed this church in those first years of its existence. What auspices more favorable could have been desired? During the forty following years in which Mr. Parsons lived and continued in this pastorate there seems to have been a condition of general prosperity with frequent additions to the membership, the whole number of names on the roll having been at the time of his death two hundred and forty-eight. But at no other time in his ministry were there so large accessions as in these earliest years.

The growth of the settlement seems to have been very rapid. Mr. Judd tells us that "The east inhabitants are not noticed in the town records of Hadley until Jan. 5, 1730, when a committee was appointed to lay out a burying-place. After 1732 the people had preaching a part of the year. In 1735 Mr. Parsons began to preach. He was called to settle April 13, 1737, and again in September of the same year. He did not accept these calls, but preached for a time in Southampton in 1737 and 1738." In 1739 the call was renewed and accepted. The first house of worship was begun in 1738. It stood where we now see the College Observatory. Services were held in this building before 1742, but it was not completed till 1753, eleven years later. This looks like slow progress, but " in 1758 the population of the settlement had become greater than that of the mother town, and in 1790 Amherst had about twelve hundred inhabitants while Hadley had only some six hundred."*

Among those who became identified with the community in its development there are certain names upon which we may fittingly linger: for they seem to have given a certain tone to this village which it has held in all its subsequent history.

I have named as one of the founders Richard Chauncey. There came with him to the settlement, his two brothers Charles and Josiah. Little is told us concerning Charles, but Richard and Josiah were men of mark, occupying responsible offices and evidently commanding the highest esteem.

Let us glance at the family to which they belonged. Their father was the Rev. Isaac Chauncey of Hadley, a graduate of Harvard College and distinguished for his erudition. An older brother and four brothers-in-law were all ministers and graduates of either Harvard or Yale. Their grandfather was Rev. Israel Chauncey of Stratford, who with his two brothers Nathaniel and Elnathan were graduated at Harvard in 1661. He was one of the founders of Yale College and was chosen to be its Rector or President, though he did not accept the election. His brother Nathaniel was the eminent pastor of the church in Hatfield, and their father was the Rev. Charles Chauncey, the second President of Harvard College. It was a family of Christian scholars, endowed with extraordinary intellectual gifts and a passion for learning. The old Stratford home contained a library unequaled, probably, by any other in private hands this side of the Atlantic. The home in Hadley, where Rev. Isaac Chauncey was pastor for forty-nine years, continued the same scholarly tastes and habits. The straitened circumstances of the family made it impracticable to send the younger sons to college, but none the less were they trained to the love of sound culture and habituated to a rare intellectual life. Three young men, brothers and companions, came from such a family and such a home to bear their part in building up this settlement and in giving it the character it was to sustain.

Notice next the young pastor, Rev. David Parsons. He also came

*Dickinson's Centennial Discourse.

from scholarly associations. His grandfather was Judge of the Hampshire County Court; his father and uncle were graduates of Harvard, which was also his own alma mater; he was a descendant of Elder Strong of Northampton, and finally a kinsman of the Chaunceys. Who can doubt the elevating influences he must have exerted during his long pastorate?

Observe again the name of Nehemiah Strong. He was a near relative of Mr. Parsons and came to Amherst soon after the organization of the church, moving hither from Northampton. We may naturally associate with him his wife's son by a previous marriage, who also came from Northampton and was afterward greatly honored here as Dea. Jonathan Edwards. Mr. Strong's two sons Nehemiah and Simeon seem to have been the first young men from Amherst who went to college. The former was graduated at Yale in 1755, the latter in the following year 1756. Nehemiah after his graduation became pastor of the church in Granby, Conn., and later professor of Mathematics and Natural Philosophy at Yale. Simeon entered on the practice of law here at home and became eminent, rising to the positions of Representative, Senator and Judge of the Supreme Court. The intellectual and scholarly traits of the family are further shown in the fact that four grandsons were graduated from Harvard, Yale or Williams.

Of similar significance is the name of Nathaniel Coleman. His son Seth Coleman was graduated at Yale in 1765, and, after studying medicine in New Haven, followed the calling of a physician in this place. Here, also, the intellectual tone of the family is proven by the superior culture of the grandchildren and the high positions they were called to occupy.

It is noteworthy that before Amherst College was founded no less than forty-two young men of Amherst families had pursued, or were pursuing, a collegiate course. In the period from 1771 to 1823, thirty-nine natives of this town were graduated at Harvard, Yale, Dartmouth, Williams and Middlebury. How are we to account for this? Whence came the impulse to this wide-spread zeal for education in such a small farming community? We turn to the influence exerted by this circle of intellectual leaders as a partial explanation of it.

But give your attention to this circle a little further. I have named six families as belonging to it. These are only the beginning. It included others like Dea. Simeon Clark—who himself and his wife were relatives of the Strongs and of Mr. Parsons,—apparently also the Boltwoods and the greater part of the old substantial families of the early settlers who lived near the center. These would naturally have come into close association as near neighbors. Thus we can see that there were the materials here for society of a high order.

But there was a peril also. People become jealous of social distinctions. And somehow the people remote from the center of this precinct seem to have become jealous of those in the village. In the winter of 1772, a little more than thirty years after the church was organized, we find "the ends of the town" combined in a struggle against the center, and this struggle was continued with great bitterness for years.

The meeting-house was now too small to accommodate the growing community, and it seemed necessary to provide more room. To meet this exigency it was proposed to build two new meeting-houses, both remote from the center; and a vote to this effect was carried by a large majority. Wrongful measures, however, had been taken to secure this result, and the injustice was so palpable that the Legislature interfered and put a stop to the proceedings.*

Immediately after this came the War of the Revolution. And here the town was divided again. We find, too, that the division, in great measure, kept along the old line. This is not altogether surprising. It was natural, perhaps, that cultivated, thoughtful men, who had always made much of the sacredness of law and the duty of loyal citizenship, should hesitate to join such an uprising,—the more because Amherst was so far from any seaport and not likely to have suffered from the oppressions of the times as many other places had done. And perhaps it was natural, too, for those who had tried to make a revolution in town affairs to enter with keen zest into this larger revolution. We can understand, also, that the animosities and antagonisms of the local strife might easily have gone into this new field and become deeper and fiercer for the vaster interests at stake.

As it was, the men who had been foremost in the scheme to divide the village, became foremost in zeal for the colonial cause, and as they had carried a majority of the people in the former contest, they now swept everything before them.

The old leaders were thus brought into disrepute, were retired from public offices and treated with no little obloquy. Doubtless they gave provocation enough for this treatment; and we cannot but rejoice that the spirit of loyalty to America triumphed so completely here in Amherst over that of loyalty to the king.

*Appendix B.

But there is a pathos in the incidents of these times which we may well heed. Remembering how these were aged men with silvered hair; that they were the fathers of the place, to which they had come in its early days and given it their best thought and warmest interest; that they were high-minded men too, scrupulous of the right, steadfast to their convictions and living in the fear of God,—remembering them thus, can we repress a feeling of regret that clouds so heavy should have gathered over them at the end?

The first pastor, Rev. David Parsons, died Jan. 1, 1781, at the age of sixty-eight. We cannot but question whether the turmoil and troubles of these later years may not possibly have hastened this event. He had been with the people in this place more than forty-five years and had seen the church and community grow from small beginnings to strength and influence. These, as they have continued for more than a century, are the best witnesses to his worth and power.

We have, however, another testimony in the "Memoirs" of one of his people, Dr. Coleman. In the journal published with these "Memoirs" the tenderest references are continually made to Mr. Parsons. In one place Mr. Coleman expresses regret that in going to college he must lose his preaching; in another he gives a sketch of a sermon and tells of the spiritual exaltation he felt in listening to it; in another of a singing school at the pastor's house "which was turned into the most solemn religious meeting he had ever seen"; in still another of the wise and sympathetic counsels he received in a visit to his pastor when under a cloud of despondency; and finally he speaks of his death in these words. "Jan. 2, 1781. Our respected, godly minister, Mr. Parsons, was removed into the world of spirits, to receive the rewards of his indefatigable labors. This providence filled my mind with anxious solicitude for my family, the church, and the people of his charge." "Jan. 4. Paid our last respects to the remains of our never to be forgotten pastor. The providence gave me lasting impressions of solemnity and engagedness in prayer." Here are intimations of the quality of the man and of his personal power over the people to whom he ministered for so long a period.

During the year following Mr. Parsons' death the war ended and peace was restored. The soldiers came back from their campaigns and the interests of the home and community rose again into prominence.

Foremost of all questions was that of a new minister. Attention turned to the son of the old minister, David Parsons the third, now known as Dr. David Parsons. He had been graduated at Harvard ten years before and had preached in Roxbury and other places. Calls had come to him to settle, but he had declined them and was disposed to follow a business life. Soon after his father's death he was asked to preach here, and finally the people invited him to the pastorate.

This action met with a strong and determined opposition. And now again, the division kept near to the old line. Especially conspicuous in the opposition were certain of the returned soldiers and many of those who had been foremost in the war party. The number engaged in it was large, too, not falling very much below that of the party in favor of Mr. Parsons. Failing to prevent the call, this body withdrew from the church and as "aggrieved" members called an ex parte council for advice.*

Meanwhile the church had called a council to ordain Mr. Parsons. This had been assigned first to Oct. 9th, but was afterward changed to Oct. 2nd and came thus on the next day after the council of the "aggrieved" met. So that council adjourned for its members to attend the ordination and met again on Friday to prepare a result and dissolve.

This result seems not to have been satisfactory, for another council was called to meet Oct. 28th, which varied somewhat in its membership from the former. In that the churches represented were Southampton, Williamsburg, Whately, Hatfield, Northampton and Westhampton, while in this they were Southampton, Montague, Whately, Hatfield and Westhampton. This council took action looking toward a reconciliation of the two parties and adjourned to meet Nov. 11th; and finally, at the adjourned meeting, advised the aggrieved party, "if their proposal of uniting in the choice of a mutual council was not complied with in four weeks to proceed to organize and settle a minister."

Our records show that the church sought a mutual council and took the necessary steps for calling one—even pressing it on the aggrieved party with great persistence. But the council was not called, and still the aggrieved did "proceed to organize."

This was the origin of the Second Church. The schism may well remind us of that in the Hartford Church which issued in the founding of Hadley. A similar strife had also arisen in connection with the separation of the Hatfield church from that of Hadley, and others

*Appendix C.

not altogether unlike these have occurred in this region in later times. Perhaps this unyielding,—is it too strong to say contentious?—disposition may have been more closely related than we think to that great love of personal liberty and that indomitable persistence in following their religious convictions which characterized the founders of New England from the time they left the mother country, and long before that. But in our retrospect we cannot but question whether these fathers might not have done their work even better than they did, if they had pondered more deeply these words of Jesus, " Blessed are the peacemakers, for they shall be called the children of God."

The pastorate of Dr. Parsons continued till Sept. 1st, 1819, a period of nearly thirty-seven years. He was then dismissed at his own request. He died May 18th, 1823.

Proofs are abundant that he was a man of remarkable abilities and highly gifted with those social qualities that make warm and constant friendships. The church greatly prospered under his care and increased in membership, notwithstanding the embarrassments with which he began his work. A new meeting-house was built in 1788 on the ground where the old one had stood and the people seem to have been harmonious among themselves and united in their esteem for the pastor.

We are to have a sketch of Dr. Parsons and of his father from a grandson who worthily represents the family to-day in the Christian ministry, and I leave to him the fuller account of their lives.

An event of no little importance during the latter part of this period was the coming of Noah Webster and his family in 1812 to make their home here. This is a proof of the attractiveness of Amherst at that time to people of culture; and this family in their coming brought reinforcements to all the better life of the community. I have no need to dwell upon the intellectual gifts of one whose name is a household word wherever the English language is spoken. But it would be a faulty sketch of the church's history if I should say nothing of his home as a center of religious life. Dr. Webster, his wife and three daughters, at their coming united with the church by letter from New Haven. Afterward two other daughters and a son united by confession of faith. The family thus gave their influence to the cause of Christ. And this influence was positive. These young ladies were active, as I have been told, especially in the revivals of their time, taking pains to seek their young friends and guide them into the new life. By reason of their intellectual and social gifts they were leaders of society and this leadership was beautifully given to the service of Christ. Individuals now living speak in terms of grateful affection concerning the interest thus manifested in their personal welfare and testify to the salutary power they exerted in the village. Probably this household was a considerable factor in giving to Amherst the religious earnestness for which it was conspicuous at the time of the establishment of the college. The Websters remained here ten years, until 1822, when they returned to New Haven. A part of the work of these years is in the great Dictionary, but there is another part whose record is above.

The third pastor was Rev. Daniel A. Clark, who had been previously settled at Weymouth, Mass. and at Southbury, Conn. He was installed Jan. 26th, 1820, and was dismissed Aug. 5, 1824.

During his time the movement which had long been preparing for the establishment of a college came to its culmination and the college was founded. In this enterprise our church bore a conspicuous and honorable part. Indeed it hardly seems an overstatement to say that the First Church was the mother of Amherst College. Dr. Parsons in his day had been reputed one of the most judicious instructors in New England and his home had been a favorite place for the faculty of Harvard College to send such students as needed to spend a time in the country. Also under his supervision and generous patronage the old Academy had been established. Thus a beginning had been made for the greater institution now proposed. To that work pastor and people alike gave their hearty zeal and united exertion, sparing no pains to start the College on its prosperous way. Of this we shall hear more fully from Prof. Tyler.

Mr. Clark was a preacher of great power. Three volumes of his sermons were published, had a wide circulation and were regarded as among the ablest sermons of the times. In one of these volumes is a biographical sketch by Rev. Dr. George Shepard of Bangor, from which I derive most of the information that I have concerning him. His style was "bold, original, pungent, direct." "His sermons were filled with thought, often original, always concisely and strikingly expressed." "He eminently excelled in Biblical instruction." "While in Amherst, he was in the maturity and full strength of his faculties; and it was here that he prepared and preached some of his ablest sermons." "Mr. Clark's person, voice, and entire manner were in perfect keeping with his style; a large masculine frame; a voice harsh, strong, capable of great volume, though not very flexible; an action, for the most part, ungraceful, but significant and natural; a countenance bearing bold, strongly marked features at every opening of which the waked and working passions would look intensely out; —altogether gave the idea of huge, gigantic power."

Again, Mr. Clark was an aggressive reformer. One of our old citizens tells me that he was especially earnest in the temperance reform and made himself unpopular by his constant agitation of the subject.

Those were the early days of the warfare against strong drink, and it cost a man something to do what the popular sentiment of a community now requires.

Mr. Clark remained in Amherst a number of months after his dismission, then became pastor of the church in Bennington, Vt.; whence he went to the First Presbyterian Church in Troy, N. Y., and after that to Adams, N. Y. He died, March 3, 1840, in New York City, and his dust was laid to rest in the cemetery at New Haven, Conn. His entries on our record book close with these words, "Here I drop my pen. May God bless the people to whom I have ministered and build them up for heaven and give them all, my friends and my foes, an inheritance among them that are sanctified."

Early in Mr. Clark's ministry the church in South Amherst was organized, Oct. 14, 1824, and four years later, at the beginning of the next pastorate, the church in North Amherst, Nov. 15, 1826. The occasion for these new churches seems to have been the growth of the sections in which they were planted. Their members went from the First Church and the Second alike, and both were weakened, though I think not seriously, by the losses thus involved.

On the 5th of January, 1826, Rev. Royal Washburn was installed as the fourth pastor, and continued in the office till his death, Jan. 1, 1833. He was married in 1817 to Harriet Parsons the daughter of Rev. Dr. Parsons, who survived her husband many years and became the wife of Hon. David Mack.

The name of Mr. Washburn is held in precious remembrance. All the allusions ever made to him in my hearing have been full of affection and praise. He combined the gifts of a good preacher with those of a good shepherd of the flock in a completeness that is unusual, and his ministry, though laborious and hampered with disease, was happy and fruitful. Prof Fiske in his Obituary Address names as conspicuous traits of his character "unaffected simplicity and modesty," "forgetfulness of self," "cautious and sound judgment," "affability and cheerfulness," "warm and generous benevolence," and to complete the whole "harmony and consistency of character." Very touching are the words Mr. Washburn uses in a farewell address to his people a little before his death. "Have you all felt, since you have thought of obtaining another Pastor, that such gifts are from the Lord Jesus? '*He* gives some Pastors.' Christian friends, have you prayed to Christ with great earnestness, that he would send you a Pastor? Listen to the last, and what you should regard as the *dying words* of your Pastor. Lay aside all division and coldness, and as a united church, loving one another, and loving the Redeemer, bow before him in humble confession and penitence, and pray with earnest importunity that he would look graciously upon you and provide you an under-Shepherd. My beloved flock, I feel unable to say much more to you, but I cannot close without entreating you to live at peace among yourselves. Let no root of bitterness spring up—it wounds the blessed Saviour, and destroys the peace and usefulness of the church. And now brethren, farewell. The God of all comfort be with you, through Jesus Christ. Amen."

In less than a year after Mr. Washburn's death the church extended a call to the Rev. Matthew T. Adam, a native of Kilmarnock, Scotland, who had been educated at Glasgow and London. He was installed Dec. 28, 1833, and was dismissed Dec. 10, 1834. His previous ministry had been under conditions very unlike those he found in Amherst and he seems to have wanted the tact to adapt himself to this New England people. For this reason chiefly his pastorate was short. At his dismission the Council testified to his personal worth as follows. "He has been unwearied in his labors, faithful and conscientious in the discharge of his ministerial duties and above all suspicion as to high moral and Christian character."

After this the church was without a pastor for over two years, and then called the Rev. Josiah Bent, who had been previously settled at Weymouth. He was installed April 19, 1837, and died in office Nov. 19, 1839. His ministry was short but fruitful and he is remembered as a faithful, consecrated man who did not spare himself for the Master or for the people whom he served in the gospel. His wife continued her membership here and her undiminished interest in the welfare of this church, till recently she passed from a life of protracted suffering to join him who had entered into rest before her.

It is fifty years ago this month that Mr. Bent died. With him closed the first century of this church's history. A half century has passed since. And in review of this, we find occasion for great joy in that all the pastors during this period, with one exception, are still living. Some of them we welcome with glad hearts to-day, to this their old field of seed-sowing and harvesting, and from others whom we had hoped to see we receive greetings warm with the interest and love of other years, which dull not with the lapse of time, nor become weakened with the creeping on of infirmities. Fathers and brethren, Colton, Dwight, Hubbell, Jenkins and Emerson, God bless them each and every one. In this place a grateful people "esteem them very highly in love for their works sake." And may it be long before we shall have to say of any of them, "They rest from their labors and their works do follow them."

But there is one recent pastor of whom even now we have to speak these words, Howard Kingsbury. How well I remember his form as I used to see him in the college choir at New Haven ! And how well you, who loved him as your pastor, remember him ! The man of gentle mold, with fine, poetic spirit attuned like a harp to vibrate at the lightest touch and make music as under the sweep of angel's hands,—too soon as it would seem to us, he went from earth "to join the choir invisible," but not too soon for you to have found out his worth and thanked God for so rare a treasure.

Concerning the story of the church during these last fifty years it seems unnecessary and superfluous for me to speak. The period has been full of life, of activities, of enterprise. But there are many here that have had a share in these and can speak of them out of their own experience. And when there are eye witnesses to testify, the man who derives his knowledge from books and hearsay may well keep silence. This is especially true with reference to personal sketches. Within the memory of those before me, many faithful men and women of remarkable gifts and eminent distinction have been connected with this church and borne a noble part in its life and work. Happily we shall be permitted to learn of them from others whose personal acquaintance will give the sketches an added excellence and vividness.

There is one conspicuous fact that I have passed over and to which I would call your attention, that is, the great revivals. I have spoken of the two at the beginning of the church's history. Follow on from that time for seventy-five years and we come upon no other awakening to compare with those. There were, indeed, seasons of religious interest, and sometimes the accession of ten or fifteen persons to the church on a single occasion. But there was no movement to stir the community as a whole. But during the last seventy-five years there have been many of these great revivals. There was one, the first, under Dr. Parsons' ministry in 1815; others under Mr. Clark in 1820 and again in 1823; others under Mr. Washburn in 1827 and again in 1831; another in 1834 during the pastorate of Mr. Bent, and three others in 1841, '45 and '50, while Mr. Colton was pastor. Here is a period of forty years during which there were no less than nine great revivals. Other revivals have come in recent years but this period is especially marked.

In a review of these awakenings, we may well observe the origin of the first of the series. There had been in this church a man of great faith and of a deeply prayerful spirit. For more than fifty years he had lived a consecrated Christian life and for more than thirty years had been a deacon here. He was now an old man, past his seventieth year, and a great longing possessed him to see such a revival as he never yet had seen. For this he prayed, and he came to have so confident a belief that his prayers would be answered that he told some of his friends that "he expected to live to witness a great display of almighty power and grace." There came a revival in 1811, but he was not satisfied. He declared that the "assurances he had received from God were not yet fulfilled." And so he prayed on till the great revival of 1815. This refreshing visited both the churches and resulted in the addition of ninety to this church alone in a single day.

In the midst of this season and with his hope at last joyfully fulfilled the good man went to his rest. Over his silent body the two churches sorrowed and rejoiced together. The pastor of the Second Church, the Rev. Nathan Perkins, preached the funeral sermon, and the old church with the new witnessed the triumph of one who had aspired to be a peacemaker and a child of God.

Such is the story of Dr. Seth Coleman's faith. You may connect it as you will with that great revival and with others that followed. You may associate with his prayers the fidelity of pastors, the sanctified culture of Christian homes like that of the Websters and the moral energy flowing from many other similar sources. But how profound and far reaching has been the influence of that one "corn of wheat which fell into the ground and died" so many years ago we can never know till all things are revealed.

And so of all the holy seed which has been sown during these one hundred and fifty years past,—or during the two hundred and fifty years since our fathers and mothers first planted themselves in New England. Think of the limitless fruitage. Behold what God hath wrought, not only here, but throughout our land and throughout the whole world.

The backward glance is chiefly valuable in helping us to understand the present and to forecast the future. It magnifies and illumines the life of to-day to connect it with those germinal beginnings from which it has unfolded. But the life of to-day holds the germinal beginnings of something larger and better still. Now, as in all former days, God's hand beckons to a kingdom that is coming. Our eyes are forward while faith and hope outrun our vision. We stand expectant for the divine thought to come out in grander meanings as fulfillment succeeds fulfillment and anticipation realized rises into keener anticipation of what is about to be. The Eternal One is our God, and in this is all promise.

Establishing here our faith, the steadfast purpose of the fathers will animate their children and from a review of their work we shall gain wisdom to stand in our places and do with fidelity what falls to our lot.

NOTE. On page 10, twelfth line from the bottom, read, " perhaps unmarried, though he seems." On page 19, fifteenth line from the top, read "*one* hundred and fifty years." On page 29, fourteenth line from the bottom, read " 1826," and twelfth line from the bottom read " 1827."

PRESENTATION OF PORTRAITS.

After the pastor's address two portraits, one of the Rev. David Parsons, D. D., and the other of his wife, Mrs. Harriet Williams Parsons, were presented to the Church by Mr. John H. Washburn, their grandson, whose father was the Rev. Royal Washburn the fourth pastor of the Church. Mr. Washburn spoke as follows:

MY FRIENDS:—

This is a part of the exercises not set down on the programme which you have in your hands, and I assure you that it is as unexpected by me as by any of you. My purpose was to send these portraits and have them placed in your hands without any further formality. And when this morning your pastor told me that I was expected to make a presentation speech and that arrangements to that end had been made, I asked him if my speech was written for me, as I was considered a fairly good reader, while I made no pretensions as a speaker. He assured me that it *was*, and that it should be given in good time. Now I am sorry to cast any reflections upon your pastor, but he has not furnished me the promised speech, and so you will be obliged to go without it.

When I was a school-boy, in one of my Speakers was a selection putting an oration in the mouth of an Indian chief (Logan I believe) in which he spoke of visiting the hunting grounds of his tribe, over which for generations his forefathers had roamed; and finding only their graves. In coming to Amherst I feel like him. In this place, where my great-grandfather, my grandfather and my father lived and labored, not one of my kindred remains, save in yonder cemetery where so many of them repose. And yet, although my kindred are gone, and though my home is far away, I love this Church, and wherever I go the memory of it remains with me.

And why should I not love the Church where my fathers labored, to which they gave their lives, and which guards their graves? May my right hand forget its cunning when I forget thee, O Jerusalem!

DR. PARSONS.

MRS. PARSONS.

In seeking to find what I might bring as my contribution to this celebration, I could think of nothing better, nothing more fitting the occasion, than the portraits of my grandfather and grandmother, Rev. Dr. and Mrs. Parsons. Of my great-grandfather no portrait exists, nor is there one of my father, but these are treasured by the family. That of Dr. Parsons is said to be an excellent likeness :—that of Mrs. Parsons I know to be so, and I take great pleasure in showing my love for this church and doing my part on this joyful occasion by presenting to you what I know you will prize so highly.

In behalf of the Church, the Rev. Dr. D. W. Marsh received the portraits and thanked the donor with these words :

For this First Church in Amherst with its memories of one hundred and fifty years, for its living officers and members I am requested to accept your beautiful gift.

These likenesses of a father and mother in your and our Israel take us back more than a hundred years, and by this venerable image of the second pastor link us to his father the very first pastor of this church. We are gratified that you have given us the picture of your grandmother as well as of your grandfather, for had there been no foremothers there would have been no family and no descendants.

The first two pastors were born *Parsons* but several of their descendants, by the gift of God and call of God's people and their own complying choice, have become parsons.

Your gift to us entitles you to honor from all. Dr. Johnson of England well expresses our indebtedness to you by saying " Whoever brings near the distant in time or space is a public benefactor." President Mark Hopkins has said that words of the fathers " fall with weight as from the height of earlier times." These silent lips are speaking now. And when all the voices of to-day shall have died away into a long silence, then, by your kindness, these lips to other generations will still speak.

In the name of the church that never dies, we thank you.

FIRST AND SECOND PASTORS.

By REV. CHARLES H. WILLIAMS.

"It is a reverend thing," wrote Lord Bacon, "to see an ancient castle or building not in decay, or to see a fine timber tree sound and perfect. How much more, to behold an ancient, noble family, which hath stood against the waves and weathers of time." These words may be fittingly applied to that family, of which the first two pastors of this church were honored representatives.

It was a prolific stock. "Few of our early settlers," remarks one historian, "are represented by more numerous families than those that perpetuate the name of this respectable stock." The Parsons tree, to borrow Lord Bacon's figure, has sent out its roots to the river and its boughs are as the goodly cedars.

Cornet Joseph Parsons, who came from England and settled at Springfield, Mass. in 1635, was the father of ten children, as was the son who bore his name. The grandson, David, had only five; but to his eldest son and namesake, your first pastor, were born nine sons and daughters, while *his* son and successor was permitted to see eleven olive-plants about his table.

Evidently, these men put faith in that word of Scripture "Children are a heritage from the Lord," and were more likely than some of their descendants to secure the blessing promised to the man who has his "quiver full of them."

That this fecundity was not limited to the Parsons stock, however, appears from an entry in the church records of Northampton; which is of interest also as showing what the clerk of that day deemed worthy of record. It relates to Mrs. Elizabeth Parsons Allen, mother of Major Jonathan Allen, who died in 1800. She was, we are told, "Eminently pious, and assisted at the birth of three thousand children."

The boughs of this tree were not only many but goodly. From the Parsons lineage have come ministers, missionaries, jurists, soldiers and men of affairs in various walks of life, who have borne themselves honorably in their several stations.

But we must not linger. Frederick Maurice reminds us that "our relation to father and mother is the primary fact of our existence, so that we can contemplate no facts apart from that." Leaving, then, the remoter ancestry, let us inquire for the parents of your first pastor. These were David Parsons and Sarah Stebbins.

Of the latter, little is known to us, save that she survived her husband nearly sixteen years, dying June 17, 1759, aged seventy-three years.

Of the husband and father we have more knowledge. The fourth son and fifth child of Judge Joseph Parsons, Jr. and Elizabeth Strong, he was born at Northampton Feb. 1, 1680—was graduated at Harvard College in 1705, taking a degree from Yale the same year—was settled over the Congregational Church in Malden, Mass., in 1709, going thence, in 1721, to Leicester in the same state, where he died in October, 1743, aged 63.

At Malden he succeeded the brilliant, but eccentric, Michael Wigglesworth.

Respecting the circumstances of his call, the historian of Middlesex Co. tells us that "it was not until after nine ministers had been considered as candidates for the pulpit, that the town and the church were able to come to a *loving agreement* in the choice of Mr. David Parsons." From another source we learn that Mr. Parsons preached, part of the day, on the first Sunday of Mr. Tufts' preaching (one whom the court, in default of prompt decision by the church, had selected as a "suitable person qualified for the work of the ministry in Malden"). It would seem that, in those days, the churches were not content with one candidate a Sunday, but must have two—a suggestive item for committees seeking a pastor, and having an "embarrassment of riches" in the way of possible candidates.

On the next day, the church met and voted to call Mr. Parsons and, on the Wednesday following the town concurred by fifty-three affirmative votes—far the greater part of the voters in the town. Inadequate support was the occasion, as with many a minister since, of his leaving in 1721, when he accepted the repeated and most urgent invitation of the church lately formed in Leicester, whither some of his parishioners had removed and were among the leading citizens.

This fact, together with the heartiness of the call, gave promise of a successful and prolonged ministry—a promise, however, which was not fulfilled. The question of finances, so often a root of bitterness between pastor and people, again came up. Mr. Parsons knew his rights and "knowing dared maintain." That they *were* his rights appears by successive decisions in his favor by ecclesiastical, legal and civil tribunals. Whether he was wise in insisting upon them, in the way and to the extent he did, we, at this distance of time and with our imperfect knowledge of the facts, are not qualified to judge. That candid and painstaking investigator, the late Rev. A. P. Marvin, writes: "The impression left by the narrative of Judge Washburn is unfavorable to the minister, but not a fact appears impeaching his character. His claim against the town was sustained by the Court of Sessions, and the town finally acknowledged it. The fact appears to be that he sought his right in a harsh and provoking way. It was folly to suppose that he could usefully minister to a people whom he had sued for the arrears of his salary, and he paid a severe penalty for his unwisdom."

The formal tie was dissolved in 1735, though doubtless the true bond of union, so far as many of the flock were concerned, had been earlier severed. Still, the minister and his family made their home in Leicester and the stone, which was over the graves of the wedded pair, is now deposited in the church building.

The eldest of their five children, and the only one of whom we have knowledge, was born at Malden, March 24, 1712, and bore his father's name. He was graduated from Harvard in 1729 and, three years later, took the Master's degree, the theme of his thesis on that occasion being "Whether all the Sacred writings are contained in the books of the Old and New Testament;"—which he answered in the affirmative. Although he began to preach at East Hadley (now Amherst) in November, 1735, he was not ordained until four years later, viz. Nov. 7, 1739, the date of the organization of the church, having meantime twice declined an invitation to the pastorate. Perhaps this prolonged courtship prevented speedy divorce and secured that permanent union which was only dissolved by his death, occuring Jan. 1, 1781, in the sixty-ninth year of his age and the forty-second of his pastorate.

His portrait has been lovingly drawn for us by the hand of a friend of fifty years, Rev. Robert Breck of Springfield, in the sermon preached at his funeral. We see him, thus, "a man of strong intellectual powers, with a penetrating eye," giving token of that shrewd and judicial mind which made his counsel valued; retaining his classical learning beyond most men of his age, but with "divinity" as his favorite study; a doctrinal preacher, reverent in manner, devout in temper and fervent in prayer. "With what solemnity," exclaims his friend, "were the morning and evening devotions offered up! I never observed anything that surpassed it."

Nor was he unmindful of the spiritual interests of his own household, while caring for the larger household of faith. "There were stated seasons daily," we are told, "wherein every one of the family was allowed, and the younger ones enjoined, to retire and pay their secret devotions to the Deity." It is said of him, also, that he was a friend to all good men, never professing friendship but where he felt it nor recalling it when bestowed.

Living in days when party feeling ran high, and sharing the opinion of the leading inhabitants of the town as to the hopelessness of the American cause, he did not, as a local historian puts it, "escape the notice of the warm friends of the revolutionary movement." In the warrant for the town meeting, January 6, 1777, the following articles appear: "To know the minds of the people of this town, whether they esteem the conduct of the Rev. Mr. David Parsons friendly with regard towards the common cause," and, "To have the minds of the people, whether they will improve the Rev. Mr. Parsons as their minister for the future."

Apparently they decided to "improve" him by a little of the "excellent oil" of reproof. For we read, further, that the town voted that the conduct of Mr. Parsons was offensive, and chose five men, two of them deacons of the church, to inform him of the fact. It was well for the comfort of the five, perhaps, that Mr. Parsons had not his father's temperament, or the interview might have been less agreeable. As it was, the relations of the pastor and people seem to have sufferred no violent strain and, four years later, death found him still at his post.

We may accept as true the words inscribed over his grave: "A man of God and faithful servant of Jesus Christ."

There follows the record of the death of Eunice W., consort of the Rev. David Parsons, who died Sept. 20, 1796, in the 94th year of her age. The sentiment appended may be taken, perhaps, as suggesting her relation to her spouse, as well as that of Christ to both: "Let me interpret for him—me his advocate and propitiation. All his works in me, good or not good, ingraft. My merit these shall perfect, and for these my death shall pay."

After the death of the father, the people called for the son, who was graduated from Harvard in 1771, studied theology with his father, was licensed to preach about 1775, and did preach with such acceptance, in Roxbury, Mass. and several towns of Conn., as to receive two or three calls. He had, however, made up his mind, owing, as is suggested by some writer, to the unsettled state of the country and his infirm health, to engage in mercantile business in his native town. But he was persuaded to supply the Amherst pulpit for a time, and, in the autumn of 1782, his health meanwhile having improved, he consented to settle as pastor, and was ordained in October of that year, resigning his charge in 1819.

As we were indebted to a clerical friend for the portrait of the father, so we turn to another, Rev. Samuel Osgood of Springfield, for a description of the son. Dr. Parsons, he tells us, "had the advantage of an uncommonly fine person, of about medium height and rather inclined to corpulency, his features regular, eyes raven black, and his whole face beaming with intelligence and good nature. He possessed social qualities of a high order. His great fluency of utterance, his fine flow of social feeling, his extensive knowledge of men and things, and his inexhaustible fund of anecdote, seemed to mark him as a leader in almost any conversation that might be introduced. His preaching was sensible and instructive, and gave you the impression that there was a great deal of reserved power. He read his sermons closely and had little or no action in the pulpit, though he was far from being tame or dull in his delivery. He had not only the keenest sense of the ridiculous, but he indulged himself in this way without much restraint." Dr. Osgood adds, however, "I believe his passion for drollery never came out in the least degree in the pulpit."

The reference to Dr. Parsons' wit is prominent in all allusions to him. Thus, in an unpublished manuscript of the late Rev. Emerson Davis, of Westfield, occurs the statement: "Dr. Parsons was an exceedingly jovial man when among his friends, full of wit and good humor. He was sensible of his fault, but seemed not to be able to discern between drollery and seriousness. When lamenting his infirmity and confessing his fault, he would often use a witticism or laughable expression to convey his idea." Very possibly Mr. Davis had in mind the anecdote, which has appeared in print, of Dr. Parsons' reply to the remonstrance of a kinsman, expostulating with him upon his too free indulgence in wit, "I know it all, Bro. Howard, and it has been my burden through life, but I suppose after all that grace does not cure squint eyes."

Dr. Parsons was an active promoter of the educational interests of the community, giving the site for the Academy and providing a bell at his own cost, serving as the first president of the Trustees of the College founded shortly before his death, and showing his loyalty to it by a substantial gift as well. For many years he had students in his family, some of whom bore testimony to the attractiveness of his home and to the charm lent to it by its head.

That Dr. Parsons had more than a local reputation is shown by facts like these. In 1788, when still a young man and only six years in the pastorate, he was chosen to preach the election sermon before Gov. Hancock and the Legislature of that year. In 1795, at the suggestion of President Dwight, he was appointed Professor of Theology at Yale, but declined the honor, chiefly, we are told, because of his warm attachment to his people. In 1800, he received the degree of D. D. from Brown University.

In 1819, as has been stated, he retired from the pastorate and, less than four years later, on the eighteenth of May, 1823, died at Wethersfield, Conn., as one of his daughters did three years before, while on a visit to his wife's kindred. His age was seventy-four years. In announcing his death, one of the religious journals of the time states: "Dr. Parsons was a clergyman of learning and talents, distinguished as an eloquent and evangelical preacher, much admired for the urbanity of his manners, and greatly esteemed and respected, by the people under his ministerial charge, as a faithful and affectionate pastor."

On the twenty-fourth of November, 1785, he had been married to Harriet, daughter of Ezekiel and Prudence Stoddard Williams of Wethersfield, and grand-daughter of Col. John Stoddard, said to have been one of the greatest men of his day. Mrs. Parsons survived her husband many years, dying here, where most of her life had been spent, on the 5th day of June, 1850, aged 84.

Of her it is enough to say that she fulfilled, in minutest detail, the picture drawn by the inspired pencil in Proverbs, of the virtuous woman, whose children rise up and call her blessed, and whose husband praises her.

Until the last decade, there has been no time since the settlement of the town that some of the Parsons family have not been among the landed proprietors, sometimes to a large extent. To-day, no one of them, I believe, owns a foot of your soil, except in yonder cemetery. But they will continue to cherish, as a priceless legacy, the memory of those Godly men who, for more than four score years, stood as watchmen upon the walls of Zion here. To you, descendants and successors of those to whom they ministered and for whom they prayed, we leave the custody of their honored dust.

RELATION OF THE CHURCH
TO THE
EDUCATIONAL INSTITUTIONS OF AMHERST.

By PROF. WILLIAM S. TYLER, D. D., LL. D.

I am asked to contribute a paper on "The Relation of the Churches to the Educational Institutions of Amherst." As the historian of Amherst College I ought to know something of the origin and history of these Institutions. And I have no hesitation in saying that the officers and members of this Church and congregation were the *founders* of Amherst Academy and Amherst College, and inasmuch as the Agricultural College was the daughter of Amherst College, this Church is the mother of them all.

It is no new thing for the Church to found and foster institutions of learning. There is a natural and mutual affinity between sound learning and true religion. God has put high honor upon learning in his Word. No small part of the Bible was written by learned men. Moses was learned in all the wisdom of the Egyptians. Paul not only sat at the feet of Gamaliel in the chief school of Jewish learning of his age, but he shows his acquaintance with Greek literature by his quotations from the Greek poets. No sooner were the miraculous gifts which signalized the first establishment of Christianity withdrawn than the Churches began to found colleges and theological schools at Jerusalem, at Alexandria, and the other principal cities, for the special purpose of raising up a pious and learned ministry who should be able not only to preach the truth but also to defend it from the assaults of its enemies.

In the Middle Ages, "The Dark Ages" commonly so-called, what light there was shone from the monasteries, which were founded by the church under the lead of such enlightened and pious princes as Charlemagne and Alfred, which kept the light both of learning and religion from being utterly extinguished, and which grew at length into the universities. As Universities appeared in Italy, in France, in England, they were established and fostered by the Church and chiefly for the better education of the clergy. Oxford and Cambridge were founded, and in the course of time enriched with princely endowments for this express purpose. Harvard College was founded by our Puritan Fathers, because, in the language of the founders themselves, they "dreaded to leave an illiterate ministry to the churches when the present ministers were dead," or, as Cotton Mather expressed it sixty years later, because "our fathers saw that without a college to train an able and learned ministry, the Church in New England must soon have come to nothing." Yale College was founded by the Congregational Ministers of Connecticut chiefly for the purpose of educating ministers for the Colony. Princeton was established by the Synod of New York for the purpose of supplying the church with learned and able ministers. All the New England colleges, and most of those which are now so thickly sown over the great West, owe their origin to Christian men and Christian motives.

Amherst College was born of the revivals and the spirit of missions that distinguished the first half of the present century, and the good people of Amherst were its godfathers and godmothers. Nay, they were its fathers and mothers. For it was, in the strictest sense, a Congregational enterprise. Amherst College was founded, not by a Presbyterian Synod, not by an Association of ministers, not by a Council of churches, but by a single local church. Other churches helped, helped freely and generously. Other ministers gave their advice and influence. But the ministers and members of this church took the lead. They bore the burden, *they* did the work. They gave the money to begin the work. They poured it out like water when money was scarce—when ten dollars was worth as much as a hundred is now—when it was more difficult to get ten dollars for a college than it is to get a thousand now. None of them were rich. Some of them literally made themselves poor by their liberal giving. They gave beyond their means. They did more than they were able to do. There were no millionaires in those days. Among all the early benefactors of Amherst College there was not a man who would be called rich now. There were very few who were considered rich then. Brethren, we testify to you of the grace of God which was bestowed upon the members of this church in that day, how the abundance of their joy and their deep poverty abounded unto the riches of their liberality: for to their power, I bear record, and beyond their power they first gave their own selves to the Lord and then gave their property to the founding of the College. The $50,000 Charity Fund which is the corner-stone, not to say the very foundation of the College, was largely contributed and wholly raised by them. In the first place they subscribed with their own hands nearly $10,000 of the first $35,000, and when the whole subscription was in danger of being rendered null and void by failure to raise the remaining $15,000, nine of them made themselves responsible by a guarantee bond for that additional sum, relying on a further subscription to reimburse them, running the risk of a failure to raise it, and in the end actually paying no inconsiderable part of it out of their own pockets. Rev. David Parsons, the second pastor of the church, headed this guarantee bond of $15,000, after having already subscribed $600 of the first $35,000. The second signer of the bond was Samuel Fowler Dickinson, a deacon and leading member of the church, who had already subscribed $600 to the Fund. The third signer was Josiah White (the father of Mrs. Edward Hitchcock), whose previous subscription to the Fund was $150. The fourth was Elijah Boltwood who had subscribed $200 of the first $35,000 and afterwards actually paid out of his own pocket $500 of the remaining $15,000. Deacon Leland (a name familiar to the older of the present members of the church first subscribed $150, then became one of the signers of the $15,000 Bond and then gave his individual bond for the unconditional payment of $1,000 of that $15,000. John Eastman (father of the Secretary of the American Tract Society, and of two excellent ministers of the gospel, and grandfather of the Misses Eastman of Dana Hall and of others who live among us) was not one of the signers of the $15,000 Bond, but he subscribed $400 to the Fund, and then actually paid $1,000 more towards indemnifying the signers. Elijah Dickinson gave the land for the site of the College buildings and the original campus, estimated at $600. Dr. Rufus Cowles gave lands in Maine valued at $3,000. Such were some of the leading donors to the foundation on which the College was originally built. And these are only examples and illustrations of the manner and spirit in which the rank and file of this church and congregation, almost without exception, contributed money according to their means and beyond their ability, for the founding of the College. And Deacon Graves, better known as Col. Graves, was the indefatigable, unquenchable, insatiable, irresistible agent, in raising almost the entire sum.

But the most remarkable manifestation of the interest, nay, enthusiasm, which the good people of Amherst felt in the enterprise was in the erection of the first dormitory, the old South College, which they, turning out in mass meeting as it were, bringing in the materials, and many of them camping on the ground, put up with their own hands from corner-stone to roof-tree in ninety days. The scene, as described by Noah Webster and other eye witnesses, seems more like romance than reality—more like a chapter from the miraculous history of the Israelites in the Old Testament, such, for example, as the building of the Tabernacle or the Temple, than an event in our Nineteenth Century. For, not only did the people have a mind to work, but they too, like the Israelites of old, felt that they were building the Lord's house. At the laying of the corner-stone, Rev. Dr. Parsons, the retired pastor and President of the Board of Trustees, performed the ceremony; Noah Webster, then vice-president and on the resignation of Dr. Parsons which immediately followed elected president of the Board, gave the address; and Rev. Daniel A. Clark, the then pastor of the church, preached a sermon suited to the occasion; and in reading the sermon and the address no thought strikes us so forcibly as the philanthropic, Christian and missionary spirit of the founders. The very title of the sermon struck the keynote of the charitable enterprise, and history herself, looking back after the lapse of almost seventy years, can hardly describe the result more exactly than in these words of faith and hope and almost prophetic vision which Rev. Mr. Clark uttered at the laying of the corner-stone:—"In vision I see it among the first institutions of our land, the younger sister and the best friend of our theological seminaries, the centre of our educational societies, the solace of poverty, the joy of the destitute, and the hope and the salvation of millions."

Morning and evening prayers were at first attended in the old village "Meeting-house," which then occupied the site of the Observatory and Octagonal Cabinet, and was considered one of the best church edifices in Hampshire County. In the same memorable sanctuary, sitting for the most part in the broad galleries, the Faculty and students worshipped on the Sabbath with the people of the parish, and often admired and rejoiced, but oftener feared and trembled under the powerful preaching of the pastor. Joseph Estabrook, the first Professor of Greek and Latin in the College, was the first Superintendent of the first Sabbath School in Amherst, and Noah Webster, who had so much to do in the founding of the College, wrote the Constitution* and was the Chairman of the Board of Managers. Professor Estabrook was succeeded by Pindar Field, a member of the first senior class. During the first ten or fifteen years tutors in college were most frequently superintendents of the Village Sabbath School and many of the teachers were college students. Tutors Burt, Clark, Perkins, Tyler and Burgess were all superintendents before 1835. Reuben Tinker of the class of 1827, one of the early missionary graduates, was superintendent during his Senior year. Henry Ward Beecher, then a senior in College, was the inspiring teacher of a large class of young men, when I was superintendent; and Thatcher Thayer, widely known among his numerous pupils as "Dominie Thayer" of Newport, was his successor. Edwards A. Beach of the class of '24 was for a year or two leader of the choir and teacher of music in the Village Church, and he told me that he "boarded round" among the good people for a part of his pay. The relations between the students and the families of the village in those early days were in the highest degree confidential and affectionate. There was none of the traditional hostility between the town and the gown. On the contrary the best families not only invited students to their receptions but boarded them, if indigent, gratuitously—if not needy, at nominal prices. And the letters which the writer received from the alumni of those halcyon days when he was writing the history of the College, (although they had already reached their three score and ten) read very much like love letters. Some of them had actually made love and found wives among the young ladies of the church fifty years before, and more recent graduates have not been slow to follow their example. College students who were teachers in the Village Sabbath School have been greatly useful in promoting revivals in the Village Church. The great revival in 1831, which was equally powerful in the college and the village, originated in the Sabbath School Concert, and owed its origin apparently to the power and pathos with which Moody Harrington of the class of '34 pressed home upon the crowded assembly the question: "Why do we sit still?"

Were there time I would gladly pursue this topic further. I have confined these hints and sketches to the first decade in the history of

*A printed copy of this Constitution, together with the record of its adoption and the first meeting of the Board of Managers, may be seen in the package of *Reports and Papers* which Mr. S. C. Carter left "to the Treasurer for posterity," and which is now in the hands of the present Superintendent, Mr. W. W. Hunt.

the College, and these might have been made fuller. I would have liked especially to sketch the lives and characters of some of the prominent men—such men as Dr. Parsons, Noah Webster, Samuel Fowler Dickinson, Hezekiah Wright Strong and Rufus Graves, who, while they were leaders in the church and parish, were preeminently the founders of the College. But I have not time to write, nor you to hear, the record of their self-denying, self-sacrificing, patriotic, philanthropic and Christian services. Besides, their biographies have already been written as part and parcel of the history of Amherst College and will doubtless occupy a prominent place in the discourses and addresses of this centennial celebration.

As the college and the town have grown in numbers and resources since the first decade, they have of necessity ceased to hold just the same intimate and familiar relations. But they have never ceased to be mutually friendly, helpful and useful. Not only have the good people of Amherst furnished a site, a home and a hearty welcome to the faculty and the students of all our educational institutions but they have always been the foremost to contribute in one way and another to the buildings, the funds and the pecuniary necessities of the Academy, of Amherst College and of the Massachusetts Agricultural College. Witness the generous subscription to the building and the books of the Library of Amherst College which, beginning as such subscriptions usually have, in the First Church and Parish of Amherst, extended to the other parishes of this and several neighboring towns, gave the College not only a new library building but a new epoch in its general prosperity, and at the same time secured to the ministers of all these parishes the right to draw books from the Library free and forever on the same conditions as the faculty and the students. Witness also the liberal contribution to the founding of the Agricultural College which the town raised by tax, and thus served itself while at the same time it subserved the interests of the Commonwealth and the cause of agricultural education. Nor can I refrain in this connection from a more particular reference to Amherst Academy, the eldest daughter of the church, of which Amherst College was an offshoot, which received its dower partly indeed from the Commonwealth of Massachusetts but chiefly from the church and the good people of Amherst—a favorite daughter, of which the mother was justly proud, for in her prime Amherst Academy occupied the foremost place among the Academies of the state, and in the year when I was connected with it as a teacher, sent thirty students to College.

most of them to Amherst. Nor must I forget to speak of the High School, the successor of the Academy, of which also Amherst may well be proud ; nor of the Grammar and Common Schools all of which she cherishes with a mother's self-denying, self-sacrificing love and care, and therein most wisely and truly loves and cares for herself, thus proving that "Self-love and social are the same." May the relations of the Church and the Educational Institutions of Amherst always be mutually pleasant and profitable, and may they never cease to illustrate the saying that benevolence is twice blessed, richly blessing the grateful receiver and blessing still more abundantly the cheerful giver. Let the church and the town ever be the atmosphere—an atmosphere of life and health and purity and peace, in which our schools and Colleges all live and move and have their being, and let the schools and Colleges ever be the vital element in that atmosphere, like the oxygen in the air we breathe, or like the sunshine which imparts light and life to every person, place and thing that comes within the sphere of its influence.

REPRESENTATIVE MEN OF THE PARISH, CHURCH BUILDINGS AND FINANCES.

By W. A. DICKINSON.

I have been asked to say what I can in twenty minutes of Representative Men of the Parish, Church Buildings and Finances.

In the very limited time at my command since the request came to me, and with the scanty and scattered sources of information within reach, I have been able to put together what amounts to hardly more than notes for a proper paper, and these not full, perhaps not always accurate, but such as it is.

The First Church in Amherst was built in the years 1867—8 and is the building in which we now are. Before that we had meeting-houses and went to meeting.

The first meeting-house was built just before 1740 when town and parish were one and the same, and was built by levy upon all the inhabitants within the town or parish territorial limits. The support of religion then was by law imperative upon every man, as much as the support of schools. The Meeting House was the Town House.

The town meeting under the same warrant considered and acted upon ecclesiastical and secular matters, raised the salary of the minister and other expenses incident to the conducting of public worship with its other monies. The leaders in the town were the leaders in the parish.

This first meeting-house stood on the hill known now as College Hill, on the site at present occupied by the College Observatory, then about the centre of the common. The vote to build it was passed in December, 1735, but work seems not to have been commenced upon it till nearly three years after, and the building not to have been finished for fifteen years more, though meetings were held in it in 1741.

It was to be, and I suppose was, nobody knows to the contrary, 45 feet in length by 35 in breadth, covered with quarter boards of spruce, corresponding to our clapboards, the roof of spruce shingles 21 inches long and without sap; the framing, which was an affair by itself, cost 19£, and it took 77 shillings' worth of rum and sugar to raise it.

There were but few pews, and these were against the walls under the galleries—for it had galleries. The males were seated together upon one side and the females together upon the other side. No likeness of the structure exists—photography was not then dreamed of, and drawing was an unpractised, if not an unknown art to the then occupants of this ground. We know it had no bell. The signal for gathering was from a conch. There was no organ, no musical instrument of any kind, no carpets, no heat or light except what came from the sun. The people came through the snow two, three, four, five miles, women riding on pillions behind their husbands or brothers, and sat through a long sermon in the forenoon, another in the afternoon, with no warmth except from the coals in the foot stoves obtained from the ample fire-places of those living near by. Mr. Parsons preached. His salary was 40£ a year—reckoned in the currency of the present about $133—and his wood; which averaged 100 loads, went sometimes as high as 120. It was raised from time to time till in 1757 it had reached $200, and in 1764 it was raised to $266.66, though if money became scarce he was to receive it in wheat at 3 shillings 7 pence per bushel and rye at 2 shillings 5 pence.

The only other expenses, except some occasional repairs, were for blowing the conch and sweeping the meeting-house, for which for many years $3 a year was paid.

In the latter part of Mr. Parsons' ministry, or in 1771, the number of inhabitants had increased beyond the comfortable capacity of the meeting-house, and the matter of enlarging or building anew began to be discussed; and then for the first time cropped out the jealousy of the centre which had gradually taken possession of some of the more ambitious and uneasy of those living further out, in all directions, and which resulted in a determined effort to divide the district—as it was then called—by an east and west line through the centre, building two new houses instead of one, and locating them, one at the north end, one at the south, making the centre the outskirts—and so far as voting went they were the winners; but to do this they must have authority from the Legislature, and here they failed; the remonstrants from the centre having little difficulty in securing an order staying all proceedings relative to building of any new meeting-house or meeting-houses in the district except upon or near where the old house stood. This was in 1773. The condition of the country was growing excited and absorbing. The war came on and nothing was done till it was over, and till December, 1787. Meanwhile in 1782, on the pretext of opposition to the settlement of the second minister, Dr. Parsons, son of the former minister, 22 members of the church from the north, south and east, more especially from the north and east, had under the lead of Capt. Mattoon, who had been in the war, was then 27 years of age, and brought back with him the temper of revolution, seceded and formed a separate parish, known as the East St. parish. There was a long tail to this and the last of it had hardly disappeared at the end of a century, but this is not the place to talk of it.

In a parish meeting held in December, 1787, it was voted to build a new meeting-house on the hill where the old then stood—that it should be set upon hewn stone—should be 65 feet long and of proportionate breadth—that it should be erected, enclosed and the lower story glazed within twelve months—and the way in which it should be accomplished was elaborately set out and provided for, and a committee of nine appointed to make all preliminary preparations—to make a particular estimate of the value of the several sticks of timber, their particular length and bigness and the number necessary to compose the frame proposed—also an estimate of the boards, shingles, sash, window frames, stuff and slit work—with a particular description of their length, bigness, and quantity, with a descriptive price affixed thereto—also of the nails and glass necessary with a price for the same—and also the number of feet of hewn stone necessary for the underpinning, with a price for the same—" and said committee are directed to divide the Inhabitants of the parish aforesaid as equally as may be into eight classes, with a descriptive list of each and every one's proportion of all and every article necessary for carrying into effect the aforementioned votes. And it shall be the duty of the committee aforesaid to assign to each class and individual of classes their respective proportion of every article which may be necessary for erecting and finishing the proposed house. The committee aforesaid are further directed to assign to the list aforesaid to each and every one his and their proportion of all labor supposed to be necessary in framing, that each class may do their proportion thereof—provided that those men proposed to be employed in framing by the classes or either of them be

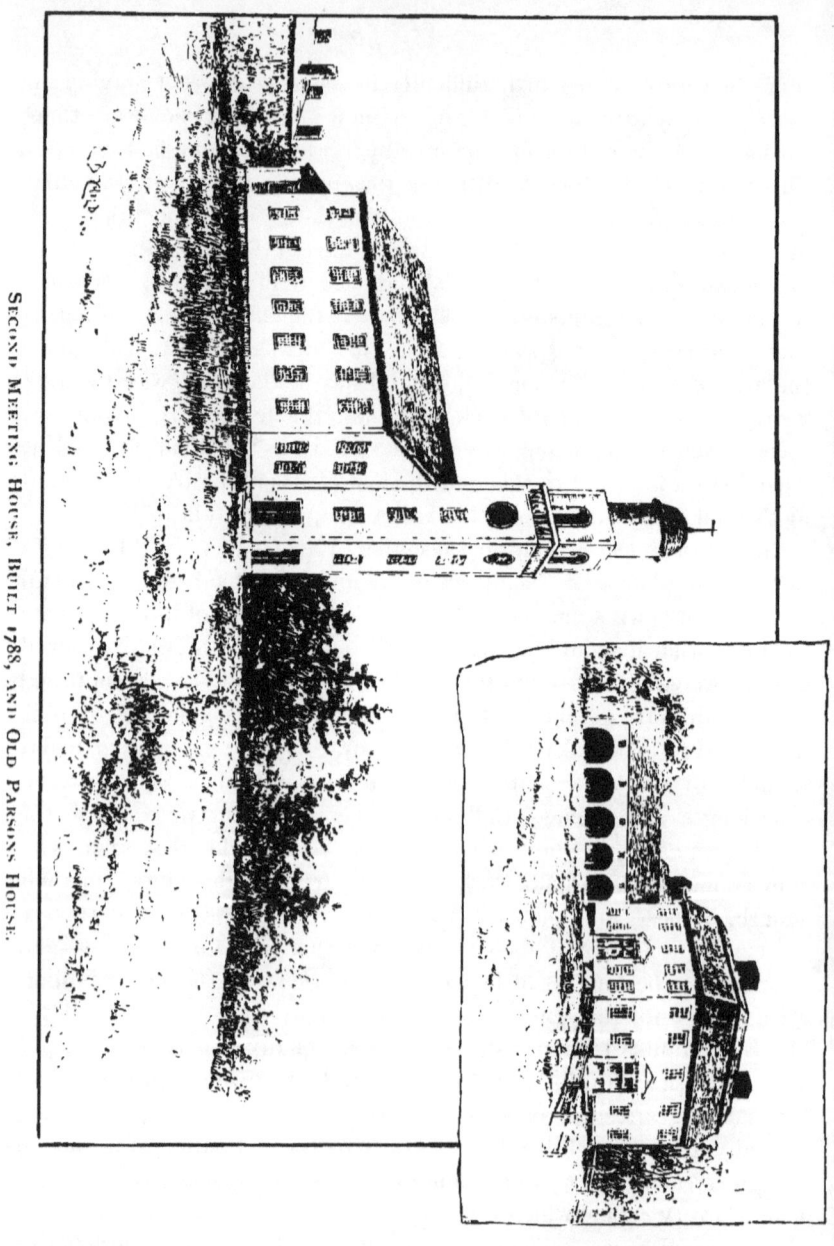

Second Meeting House, Built 1788, and Old Parsons House.

approved by the master of the frame." And very much more, in detail. The Building Committee was not selected till the May following and consisted of Simeon Strong, Esq., Capt. Eli Parker, Elijah Dickinson, Daniel Kellogg and Zebina Montague.

June 18th it was voted to take the old house down the next Monday, and a committee of five appointed to superintend it—but to be taken down without cost to the parish—another committee of three to take care of the timber and dispose of the old stuff which could not be used in the new house—and that the spectators be served on raising days at the frame with cake and cheese and liquor at the parish expense—that the meeting-house committee appoint such a number of men as they think proper to wait on the spectators—and that the raisers have a good and decent entertainment made for them at the parish expense.

In September leave was given to individuals by subscription to build a belfry over the porch proposed to be built on the west side of the meeting-house; and this appears to have been done, for in July, 1791 they voted to finish the internal part of the belfry in a decent manner, with two flights of stairs from the lower floor to the first landing place, and that the present standing committee be a committee to effectuate the above vote; and 40£ was appropriated for the purpose.

They got into the house to hold a parish meeting in November, but the galleries were not put in till the next summer, and the inside was not finished until 1791, under a contract made with Mr. Samuel Abby Dec. 31st, 1789; who in a long and carefully worded paper agreed to finish it in a decent and elegant manner, and within two years; for which the parish stipulated to give him 20 bushels of rye at three shillings to the bushel, and twelve bushels and a-half of Indian corn at two shillings and five pence by the bushel within one month, and two barrels of pork as pork is barreled for market within one month and to be paid three hundred and sixty pounds, deducting therefrom the price of said grain and pork, the said sum to be paid in the following manner, that is to say, one hundred pounds to be paid in cattle or grain, cattle to be delivered at the value in money by the fifteenth day of October next, grain to be delivered at usual price by the first day of February in the year 1791—another hundred pounds to be paid in cattle or grain at the like prices—cattle to be delivered by the fifteenth day of October, 1791, grain to be delivered by the first day of February, 1792; the residue of the three hundred and sixty pounds to be paid within one year after the work shall be completed—with interest from the time that the work shall be completed until paid.

In January, 1792 it was voted to raise four pounds to procure a "cushing" for the pulpit, and in December, 1794 to raise four pounds to dress the pulpit in addition to the four pounds that was granted in 1792 for the "cushing."

In December, 1792 it was voted to raise a hundred pounds to buy a bell, and in April, 1793 to pay Mr. Samuel Abby an additional fifty pounds to the first contract for his cost in finishing the meeting-house, and by this time, I believe, they considered it somewhere near done, though they added what they styled a cupola to it as late as 1815 at an expense of $100—and then it was considered one of the finest meeting-houses in the region.

It was entered by doors on three sides, south, east and west. The pulpit was on the north, in the centre of one of the broad sides, about on a level with the gallery; over it hung the sounding-board. The deacons' seat directly under and in front, where the deacons sat facing the audience. The singers occupied the long gallery opposite; the boys the one on the right and the girls that to the left—this from 1801. Tithing-men were appointed to keep them in order, and often, it is said, themselves made as much disturbance as if engaged in quelling a riot.

I do not find the vote in the Amherst records, but in Hadley the town voted that there should be some sticks set up in several places in the meeting-house with some fit persons placed by them, and to use them as occasion shall require to keep the youth from disorder." That the sticks were used here is within the memory of some now living.

This was the status at the time the college was established in 1821. Providing seats for the accommodation of faculty and students wrought considerable change, and out of the new conditions in the course of a few years more the question of a new place of worship was often up; and at a parish meeting held Tuesday, January 8th, 1828, a vote was passed to build a new house, provided sufficient funds for the purpose could be raised by a previous sale of pews, a committee appointed to take the matter into consideration, and report at an adjourned meeting. The committee were Elijah Boltwood, Enos Baker, Lucius Boltwood, Horace Kellogg, Elijah Nash, John Lealand and David Dexter, and they reported nine days after, Jan. 17, advising to build, and to build on land offered by the college, 10 rods square, on the north-east corner of the farm lately owned by the heirs of the Rev. David Parsons. They also brought in a plan of a building 80x65 feet, with 124 pews on the ground floor, the cost of which they estimated at $6,500; and in further pursuance of their instructions they reported a series of regulations to govern the management of the property, among them one that

"The parish shall have no right to allow town meetings to be held in said house."

These had always been held in the old house, and there had been no other place.

Another that

"No person shall sell or lease his or her pew to any black or mulatto—or to any person of infamous character—or shall in any way alter or deface the external appearance thereof."

The report of the committee was adopted without qualification or amendment, plan, regulations and all, and the meeting was adjourned to the next Tuesday, 22nd, for the sale of pews. On coming together at that time they voted to adjourn immediately to Boltwood's Hotel, and then the sale commenced with Col. Smith for auctioneer. This was after a while adjourned to the next Monday, 28th, to meet at the same place, then to Feb. 11th, then 25th, then to March 13th, then 20th, when for some reason which does not appear, the sale was begun anew, with Luke Sweetser auctioneer, and proceeded till at the adjournment pews had been bid off to the amount of $5,427. April 21, with those sold at private sale between times, the footing reached $6,635; something more than the estimated cost of the building.

The new house was commenced. Col. Howland was designer and builder, and had it finished in season for the commencement exercises of 1829. It was a substantial structure, is still, and may have fulfilled the hope and purpose of the building committee; though architecturally it could hardly have been thought an inspiration even then, and the discussions were many among the students as to the age and order which it represented. It was more commonly classed as Tuscan, that being the most elementary described in the books; but by some to be back of books—ancient Egyptian. This was the claim of Tutor March of the class of 1845, while one of the French professors in the early days pronounced it the Eighth Astonishment. Originally it had a large portico in front, supported by giant pillars standing upon a stone platform. Otherwise it was much the same as now. Inside the pulpit was a close box reached by a long flight of narrow stairs on either side, though about 1840 this was taken down and a really handsome mahogany affair substituted. The pews all had doors, and every man was buttoned tight in. The high-sided pews for the blacks and mulattoes were located in the further corners of the house, over the gallery stairs.

Stoves seem not to have been introduced till 1833, for in December of '32, according to the records, a committee was appointed to see if means could be provided for heating the meeting-house, and at a meeting held on the 31st of the same month it was voted that

"Consent be and hereby is given to place stoves in the meeting-house provided that they can be purchased and put up by subscription." And even then they seem to have been set in what we should call the vestibule; for in 1835; two years later; it was voted to remove the partition wall in the space of the meeting-house for the purpose of enclosing the stoves in the body of the house. As I remember them they stood within this circular wall, the pipes running the whole length of the side aisles directly over the centre, entering the chimneys at the west end, with tin troughs underneath to catch the creosote which dropped from the joints.

The basement was finished off after a fashion, and was used for town meetings, agricultural fairs, courts, auctions and other entertainments. Not for all other, however; for in 1838 it was voted that the third article in the warrant relative to granting the use of the meeting-house for the purpose of holding lectures on the subject of slavery be dismissed.

The same year individuals were given the privilege of erecting horse-sheds in the rear of the meeting-house, subject to the discretion of the parish committee.

In 1839 the old and first bell which had somehow been injured, was exchanged for a new and larger one—the one now on the Baptist church.

Down to 1862 this bell rang at noon and at 9 in the evening as notice for dining and retiring. At this time the evening bell was discontinued—but the noon not for some years more.

In 1839 too came the acquisition of the first musical instrument ever owned by the parish, a double bass viol. With my first recollection Josiah Ayres managed it, and the tones he drew from its lower chords in his accompaniment to the singing of some of Watts' Favorite Hymns, haunt me even now. Such lines as

"That awful day will surely come,"

"That last great day of woe and doom."

and

"Broad is the road that leads to death," etc.,

seemed to me sufficiently depressing in plain print: sung with the accompaniment, they were appalling—to a boy.

Our next great move was in 1854—5, when the lecture room—as it was called—was built, just west of the meeting-house: a modest, tidy structure of wood, plain, white, perhaps a little cold, but adapted to its purposes.

In the same period we rose to a small second-hand organ. There was a great deal of doubt about this: there was a suggestion of Rome and Episcopacy in this instrument not brought up by the double bass viol, but some of the young people were very urgent, and it was decided to let it be tried.

Things were running now on rather a high key, but the hunker element held in till 1857, when it was proposed to raise seventy-five dollars to purchase four kerosene chandeliers to light the meeting-house. This was too much, a step too far for those who held religion rather as a matter for the practice of fine economy. They said it portended the theatre: they thought—as some of us believed—it would add to the burden of maintaining public worship; and threats of signing off were loud if the unsanctity were persisted in; the air was thick; there was concern on the part of the movers in the project and hesitation, but somehow the breakers were cleared and the chandeliers hung.

In 1861 we had so far recovered from the shock of this innovation that we bought the old Shepard house for a parsonage, paying, or giving a parish note for $2,500 for it; and all was proceeding quietly and peaceably, despite occasional talk of the need of thorough repairs and additions to the meeting-house, or building entirely anew, and ineffectual efforts in parish meetings to bring something in this direction to pass, till about 1864 when the question became more pressing and would not down. The story of the numberless meetings from that time on for the next two or three years, the different plans and sites proposed, varying views, till the adoption at last of the plan we followed—is full of interest but too long and the facts too recent to be recited here. Under the Lord's guidance, the stimulus of Mr. Jenkins' preaching and personality was the largest factor in the result, and yet the greater proportion of the people did their full part and did it cheerfully. It was accomplished not without effort, not without opposition, not without sacrifice: but the effort did us all good, and most those who did the most: for it is not what we hold back but what we give out that enriches us. The entire property cost in round numbers $880,000. We entered upon it with parish notes out to the amount of $838,500. To make sure of the extinction of these a few persons contributed together the sum of $10,000 for a sinking fund to be used whenever it should have increased sufficiently for this purpose. This fullness of time was reached during the last year, and this church, built by our fathers and their children, is now without debt. It stands here for the faith that is in many of us, for the hope and earnest aspiration that is in all; it is our continuing confession, and unceasing prayer. Would that the fathers who sleep were with us to-day—that row who sat one behind the other on the north aisle.

At the head, Luke Sweetser, for a generation exercising the largest influence in the affairs of both church and parish; a successful business man, of bright and active mind, genial manner, a generous host, conscientious, believing religion a chief concern, hesitating before no duty as he saw it, conservative to a degree that commanded the confidence of those who saw safety only in the old ways, yet too intelligent not to be open to suggestions for improvement, and when convinced, ready and helpful in carrying them into execution; not the first or among the first to feel the importance of a more fitting house of worship, but second to none when he came to it, in the time, energy and devotion he gave to making the undertaking a success.

Edward Dickinson, proud of being of Amherst soil, of the sixth generation born within sound of the old meeting-house bell, all earnest, God-fearing men, doing their part in their day toward the evolution of the Amherst we live in; in the front from earliest manhood, prompt with tongue, pen, time, money, for anything promising its advancement, leading every forward movement, moral or material, in parish and town; holding many positions of trust and responsibility, never doubted, the soul of integrity and honor, fearless for the right, shirking no duty, and dying at his post as representative of his district in the Massachusetts Legislature where, in his seventy-second year, he had gone to help in shaping the legislation proposed affecting the interests of the Central railroad.

L. M. Hills, who had but lately joined us, and joined with the distinct purpose of lending his strong hand to the carrying out the plans then in contemplation; his coming, indeed, being the element which determined the shape they took, and counted upon to make them certain; a sturdy man to look upon and of sturdy qualities, square and honest in all his dealings, resolute, self-reliant, of ample means of his own creation; without these three men this church could not have been built; with either of them indifferent it could not. Their combined strength, influence and following only made it possible.

Next in the row, perhaps next in importance, William Cutler, representative of one of the old and prominent families, the then leading merchant in the village, naturally slow and cautious, more apt to see objections than advantages—the course of events never quite to his mind—finding much to condemn, little to approve outside Daniel Webster and the old Whig party, but who went into the new church enterprise with a spirit that seemed almost like a revolution of himself, and carried many with him from the back seats, where the greatest confidence was felt in him, whom no one else could have moved.

Then Sidney Adams, a life-long neighbor and friend of Mr. Cutler's, just his opposite in make-up, amiable, seeing only the sunny side, useless in a tempest, but using a good oar in smooth water, always interested in the line of the best, and winning others to it by his pleasant, affable words and ways, and who gave his whole heart to this, as he thought and as it proved, the last great work in which he was to have a part.

But the membership of this parish has included strong and earnest men all through, and the names most prominent in the beginning, when town and parish were the same, are in good part those most familiar to us now. The Bakers, Boltwoods, Clarks, Churches, Cowles, Dickinsons, Eastmans, Hawleys, Kelloggs, Montagues, Smiths, Strongs. With these were the Chaunceys, Colemans, Fields, Ingrams, Nashes, Porters, Warners, who, so far as I know, are unrepresented among us now.

John Ingram headed the first petition of the people residing in what is now Amherst, to the General Court, to be made a separate precinct; the main object being to provide in the legal way for calling and supporting a minister of their own. This was not successful, but a second petition, headed by Zachariah Field, only six months later, was granted and the precinct boundaries fixed as the petition asked.

The first meeting of the precinct was held at the house of Zachariah Field October 8, 1735, when Samuel Hawley was chosen moderator, John Nash clerk, Ebenezer Dickinson, Aaron Smith and John Nash assessors, and John Ingram, Samuel Boltwood and Samuel Hawley committee to call precinct meetings.

At this first meeting they voted to hire a minister half a year and to build a meeting-house; chose John Ingram, Jr., Jonathan Cowls and Dr. Nathaniel Smith to hire a minister, and Samuel Boltwood,

Ebenezer Dickinson, John Cowls, Pelatiah Smith and John Ingram, Jr., to build the meeting-house.

The precinct was made a district—an advance—in 1754—Josiah Chauncey being the agent appointed by the precinct to appear before the General Court and urge the same.

The first meeting of the district was held at the meeting-house March 19 of that year, when Deacon Ebenezer Dickinson was moderator, Josiah Chauncey clerk, and Joseph Eastman treasurer; Deacon Ebenezer Dickinson, Jonathan Dickinson, John Dickinson, Dr. Nathaniel Smith and Moses Dickinson, selectmen; Ebenezer Dickinson, Jonathan Dickinson and Moses Dickinson, assessors; Gideon Dickinson, Daniel Dickinson, Nathaniel Dickinson, Ebenezer Mattoon and Jacob Warner, surveyors.

The parish, as a parish, was organized not till 1783, under a call for a meeting for that purpose issued by Nathaniel Dickinson, when he was chosen moderator and his son Nathaniel clerk. At this meeting the general committee chosen were Capt. Eli Porter, Dr. Eleazer Smith, Martin Kellogg, Lt. Joel Billings and Thomas Hastings.

I give the names of the men holding the offices under the several organizations because in those days the people were willing and glad to choose their best men to serve them and the best men were willing and esteemed it honorable to serve. It is impossible within the limit assigned me to speak a separate word of all the really marked men. A few of the more constantly active and conspicuous were:

Ebenezer Dickinson, grandson of the first Nathaniel who came from England in 1630, landed at Boston, settled in Wethersfield, was one of the five sent forward by the fifty-nine who met in Hartford in April, 1659, and engaged to transplant themselves, if God permit, to the plantation purchased on the east side of the river of Connecticut, beside Northampton, to lay out for them fifty-nine home lots; the first Deacon here, as his grandfather had been there, one of the committee of three whose names appear upon the call to the first Mr. Parsons to settle here; a man of serious nature, confident, direct, without doubts, with a natural aptitude for affairs, active, and always present in everything pertaining to the welfare of the church or community.

John Nash, of the same date, general style, and sterling qualities, associated with Mr. Dickinson as Deacon, on the committee to call the first minister, carrying always a full share of the duties and responsibilities of the time—few and simple to be sure, compared with those of the present—both were of the pure puritan type, of the kind for foundation men.

In the same line Elisha Smith, Lt. John Field, Solomon Boltwood, Josiah Chauncey, who was in almost from the start, and one of the most independent, talented and facile of the early settlers, a believer in this world as well as the next; son of Rev. Israel, second minister of Hadley; great-grandson of Rev. Charles, president of Harvard College; and his grandfather was offered the presidency of Yale, but declined. He was Capt. of militia under the Crown, was the first justice of the peace in Amherst when that office meant something, in 1758, and had the distinction of being the first man chosen from Amherst to the General Court, in 1760, and again in 1762, when Hadley, South Hadley, Amherst and Granby together chose but one representative, and the first man chosen to represent the whole district not a resident of the old village of Hadley.

The precedent was over-ridden a second time in the election of Simeon Strong to the same office in 1767 and 1769—he had been commissioned as justice of the peace in 1768—he was a graduate of Yale in 1756, the first professional lawyer in the town, and as such consulted and employed in all matters involving legal knowledge and action; rose to eminence, and at the time of his death in 1804 was associate justice of the Massachusetts Supreme Court. He built and lived in the house at present occupied by Mrs. Emerson, on Amity street.

Seth Coleman, whose name appears upon about every page of the parish records from 1785 to near the time of his death in 1816, and who was clerk and treasurer of the parish continuously from 1785 to 1808, was a graduate of Yale in 1765, a carefully educated physician, a man of scholarly and refined tastes, with more spirituality than most of those about him, whose interests and energies outside his profession seem to have centered largely in matters pertaining to the church, where his influence was always elevating. He lived in the old-fashioned, yellow house, built by his father, Nathaniel Coleman, on the lot just north of Dr. Bigelow's present residence, on North street, then eight or ten feet above the present level, a beautiful, natural mound, which escaped the march of improvement till sometime after 1840.

Eli Parker, born in 1746, living till 1829, was in at the first and among the foremost, having a part in everything which was going on about him. He was a military man, too, and he, with Reuben Dickinson, were the two active captains from Amherst in the Continental army.

Moses Dickinson, born in 1718, who lived to be eighty-five, equally prominent in affairs of church and state, at the head of almost all the important committees, including that of the standing committee of correspondence with the Boston committee just before and early in the war; delegate from Amherst to the various conventions of the time, and representative to the General Court; second to none in the best qualities of citizenship. His son, Elijah, not the equal of his father but with many of his qualities, and a man of importance; was a colonel in the State Militia. He built the house where John White now lives, just south of the college, owned that farm, and gave from it the land where all the earlier college buildings were erected.

Ebenezer Boltwood, graduate of Harvard in the class of 1752, merchant, a man of quiet tastes but public spirit.

Daniel Cooley, an educated man also, delegate to the first convention that met in Boston in 1788 to consider the proposed United States Constitution, representative to the General Court, and serving the town in various other capacities.

Nathaniel Dickinson, Jr., who perhaps was the most virile and popular Amherst man of his generation to Amherst men, unless the honors may have been even between him and Ebenezer Mattoon, who greatly resembled him in many ways: the one a graduate of Harvard in '71, educated as a lawyer; the other a graduate of Dartmouth in '76, both high-spirited, bold, defiant, of the precise mould and mettle for revolution, and entering into it with a zeal to delight the heart of old John Adams; holding every manner of office, never out of it, Dickinson holding to the civil line, Mattoon being also quite a figure in the military:—the traditions of these men, their peculiar independence and freedom from the restraints of conventionalism under provocation, are fuller than of any of their contemporaries.

Zebina Montague—and Luke his cousin; in business together, their store standing directly across the present Main Street in front of the Montague place, where Luke lived; Zebina in the house built by himself, just around the corner, and destroyed by fire in the blizzard of March, 1888, where the new Town Hall stands; Luke rather an indoor man; Zebina giving his time to the public; a captain, colonel and general in the militia, and representing the town ten years, nine consecutively, in the Legislature.

Enos Baker, father of Alfred, Osmyn, George and Enos.

William Boltwood, father of Lucius.

Dr. Robert Cutler, the leading local physician of his time, greatly esteemed and beloved.

Noah Webster, whose fame is coextensive with the English language—was a resident of Amherst but ten years, 1812 to 1822, but in those years no man was a larger part of it than he. Notwithstanding the drain upon his time and strength by his literary and philological studies, he neglected no duties of citizenship; was alive to every public interest, always in parish meeting, always in town meeting, moderator frequently of both; represented the town three years in the Legislature; wrote addresses for a variety of occasions, as he was called upon; setting an example which might be followed to advantage by our literary and professional men of the present day. He was a general favorite with all classes.

Samuel Fowler Dickinson; familiarly called Esq. Fowler; who stood in the forefront in the Amherst of his generation; a fine scholar; a lawyer of distinction and wide practice; a man of rare public spirit, the highest moral purpose, unflagging zeal; the leader in every local enterprise; holding many offices of trust, a dozen years and more a member of the Massachusetts Legislature, in both houses; of the most earnest and active religious faith and life, a deacon at twenty and for forty years thereafter, one of the leading founders of the college, sacrificing for it his property, time and professional opportunities, in the idea of getting the Gospel sooner to the ends of the earth.

H. Wright Strong, son of Judge Simeon Strong; lawyer by profession, but without disposition to confine himself to the drudgery of practice; liking a more open field, with freer play and greater variety; attracted to the new, and larger; sanguine, energetic, tireless in pushing whatsoever he had enlisted in; his home a centre of graceful and refined hospitality; ranked by Prof. Tyler in his history as standing with Mr. Dickinson as one of the "three working founders" of the college. In the latter part of his life, postmaster under both Jackson and Van Buren.

Dr. Rufus Cowles, graduate of Dartmouth in 1792; large landowner, a sort of natural baron; bluff, hearty, generous; full of force and of the unrestrained individuality so prevalent in his time; at the front and with the best in everything affecting the prosperity of Amherst; owned and lived in the house on North Street at present occupied by L. D. Cowles—he is remembered traditionally by his hostility to the introduction of stoves into the meeting-house, on the ground of their vitiating the air, and his peculiar way of exhibiting it.

David Parsons, son of Dr. Parsons, full of the Parsons quaintness and oddity, startling at times in the bluntness of his expressions.

Calvin Merrill, who built the house on the east side of the common known now as the old Merrill house; and John Eastman, men less demonstrative, taking less room, but no less efficient; not captains, but most faithful lieutenants.

Joseph Church, Jr., too, working close by their side.

Dr. Isaac G. Cutler, inheriting the talent and practice of his father.

These reach through the old regime, the four-score years of the Parsons', and bring us to comparatively modern times, or about the time of the establishment of the college. Some of them into the new period; one of them, the elder Dr. Cutler, is kept fresh by the anecdote told of him, that selected for his great courtesy, suave manners and his years to carry to Dr. Clark, successor to Dr. Parsons, some complaints made of him, among others the length of his sermons, when Dr. Clark answered that he was commanded to preach the Gospel, he replied, that he understood that fact, but that they didn't want it all at once.

Among those who have stood for the most in later years, the names of John Leland, Lucius Boltwood, Simeon Clark and David Mack should be added to the previous roll.

Deacon Leland, as we always called him, for he was deacon here 30 years, moved here from Peru in Berkshire County, where his father was minister, in 1820, and at once identified himself with everything here; was an intelligent, liberal, public-spirited citizen, prompt to help in whatever promised to advance the interests of town, education or religion; he was one of the early friends and benefactors of the college, was its first treasurer, was among the most helpful in securing the first railroad into Amherst, and served some years for Amherst in both branches of the Massachusetts Legislature.

Lucius Boltwood, grandson of Solomon Boltwood, one of the first settlers; was a lawyer, of considerable property; another of the early friends of the college; secretary of the Board of Trustees for many years, Commissioner of the Charitable Fund also; familiar with every page of its history, and rendering it much and valuable service; of a great deal of manner, overflowing with good humor, remembering everything he ever heard, and with slight prompting from Mrs. Boltwood everything that ever occurred; of sincere convictions and the courage of them; one of the original abolitionists and I think the first candidate of the old Liberty party for Governor; a staunch parishioner; liking all improvements, and ready to do his part in them.

Simeon Clark, with two generations behind him of the same name, long time deacon, was one of the modest men, of more than ordinary intelligence, whose candor, good judgment and practical christianity, with his faithfulness to every duty, made his opinions always sought and respected even by those mentally his superiors. He was one of the permanent factors in all church and parish affairs, and in those of the town as well.

General Mack was a man to command attention anywhere, tall, erect, of powerful build, with a fine head finely set, clear, exact, just, a believer in law and penalty for its breach ; strong as a lion, pure as a saint, simple as a child, a Puritan of the Puritans : I remember my first sight of him—I was four years old—I thought I had seen God. He was moral and spiritual tonic to any community he entered.

There are others in number whom it would be a pleasure to recall did time permit. Characters used to be more plenty than they are now.

There was Kies Eastman, worthily bearing one of the best old family names ; living upon his farm a mile to the north ; a director in the old Amherst Bank.

Alfred Baker, founder of the Hampshire Agricultural Society.

Tim Henderson, Chester Kellogg—clouds fled before their cheer.

Judge John Dickinson, with his kingly haughty head.

The portly form of Cotton Smith.

Billings Green, pure minded, sweet hearted.

Good Deacon Gaylord.

S. C. Carter, alert, bright, a sunny face and pleasant word for everyone ; always full of statistics, ready and helpful everywhere ; a youth in heart at eighty.

Sam Nash, direct descendant of Dea. John Nash, brightest minded of all the generations of Nash ; brought up a farmer ; making himself an editor ; something of a politician of the better sort ; respected for his talent, his enterprise and his aims ; founded the *Hampshire and Franklin Express*, from which, in a narrower field, the *Amherst Record*.

The Hawleys, over there, Hezekiah, Zachariah and Levi.

The Cowles's, Silas and David and Daniel and Elijah, all good and true men.

Long-time Deputy Sheriff Palmer, honest as the day, and in the duties of his office the best posted deputy of the county.

Dr. Gridley, that strange, queer, eccentric, fascinating man ; doctor, politician : hated, admired, distrusted, believed to carry life in his band; apparently not knowing day from night, that Sunday came the same day every time, his own house from another's; who wouldn't go straight if he could go across; regular only in being irregular; a most picturesque character.

But I must stop somewhere—and it might as well be here.

The change and progress from the first rude wooden meeting-house on the hill to the fair proportions of this stone church on the slope, fairly measure the growth and progress in wealth, taste, possibly culture, in the town and in the country all through, in the same time.

Has manhood gained—is that more vigorous, purer, loftier now than formerly? Is it up to the best that has been? Granting that the highest standard and type exist—we cannot fail to perceive that we are counting fewer and fewer in numbers of the kind of men that save cities. The tendency to centralization—increasing constantly in the last fifty years—drains the country of its most enterprising sons, and is reducing it to much the same condition in this respect as the drafts for the civil war reduced the South.

Those independent, strong characters—men of mark—who used to be scattered over our hills—ministers, lawyers, doctors—are not to be found there now. They are at the front—in the cities—in the struggle for wealth and power and fame—a struggle as fierce and desperate as the struggle of battle.

This is inevitable in the nature of things for the present—it may not always be so. While it is, the town or parish of this size that holds its own is the exception, and must be surrounded by most favoring circumstances. We should not have done this here, if indeed we have—if it had rested with the men alone.

But the women count in our modern census. They have appeared above the surface in the last generation, and become a power, nowhere more than in parish affairs, where they have found a congenial field for their activities and displayed them to good advantage. We no longer go home and tell them what we have done at parish meeting; they tell us what they have done at the sewing society. They are hardly longer the power behind the throne; they are a good part of the throne itself.

It is not quite easy for a masculine man to admit all this; but if he will live in the country, he might as well—and thank God for salvation even so.

MATERIAL PROGRESS OF ONE HUNDRED AND FIFTY YEARS IN AMHERST.

By HENRY F. HILLS.

One hundred and fifty years ago (1739) there were only 29 householders or settlers here, as follows:

Joseph Clary,	Samuel Hawley, Jr.,
John Ingram, Sr.,	Ebenezer Dickinson.
Ebenezer Kellogg,	Joseph Wells,
John Ingram, Jr.,	Jonathan Atherton,
John Cowles,	Samuel Boltwood,
Zachariah Field,	John Nash,
Samuel Boltwood,	Aaron Smith,
Samuel Hawley, Sr.,	Nathaniel Smith,
Joseph Hawley,	Richard Chauncey,
Charles Chauncey,	John Perry,
Stephen Smith,	Nathaniel Church,
Nathaniel Smith,	Ebenezer Williams,
William Murray,	John Morton,
Nathan Moody,	Moses Smith.
Pelatiah Smith.	

These 29 householders had 35 ratable polls and were in possession of 19 horses, 39 oxen, 52 cows and a few swine.

They altogether had 350 acres of improved land, or land that had been cleared of the original forest, and there were six non-resident land owners whose lands under cultivation aggregated 43 acres.

All of the improved land in town, in the year 1739, amounted to no more than 400 acres, or a tract just about the size of the Agricultural College farm. Ebenezer Kellogg was the largest landholder at that time, holding 48 acres.

I am indebted to Mr. C. O. Parmenter for valuable assistance in the preparation of this paper.—H. F. H.

Now, instead of 350, there are more than 16,000 acres of improved land, and 1,329 persons are assessed, upon a real and personal valuation of $3,238,000.

Our farmers boast of more than 1,400 of the finest dairy cows, and every week several tons of the choicest butter are made by two successful creameries.

In 1783 there were five taverns and eight other places for the sale of intoxicating drink in Amherst—with not more than 700 inhabitants. Besides these, there was a distillery in the ravine (back of President Seelye's residence) where 3,000 barrels of cider were made into brandy yearly. Surely we have made progress in the matter of temperance.

The first recorded vote to build school-houses was in 1761, but none were built until 1764, owing to quarrels as to location.

The year 1765 marks the establishment of the first public school in town, and the appropriation was about $100. In that year Josiah Pierce, a Harvard graduate, opened a school on the 27th of October, and taught six months in the year "*between the* MIDDLE *school-houses*," the expression probably meaning that he divided his time between school-houses in East and West Streets. It must be remembered that he taught boys only, girls not being allowed to attend school at that time, nor for years after.

The city of Boston did not admit girls to the public schools until about 1700, and Northampton, now proud of its college for young women, with nearly 500 students, did not think it proper for girls to attend the public schools until about 1802.

Schoolmaster Pierce with a college education could command but $5.33 per month as compensation, and was obliged to teach a "ciphering school" during the winter, at one shilling per evening; also to preach as opportunity offered, at 18 or 20 shillings per Sunday.

That he failed to live sumptuously is inferred from the record, for it says, "He dismissed his school in disgust, March 29th, 1769."

Such is the record of the first attempts at public school education in town; and we need only to point to our present public school system, with an annual appropriation of $8,000 to $10,000,—and to our public school-houses scattered at convenient points about town,—with our school superintendent and corps of well-equipped and well-paid teachers, and 700 pupils in attendance,—to convince the most sceptical of the progressive strides which we have made since Josiah Pierce gave up his work in disgust 120 years ago.

In 1814, Amherst Academy began its educational work, and "obtained a reputation second to none in the State."* "It attracted pupils from every part of New England," but became more local in its work, and finally gave way to the high school.

In May of the year 1820, work was begun upon the Amherst College buildings. The contest for location had been severe and persistent, but the people of Amherst won then, as, in 1867, they did in the struggle for the location of the Agricultural College.

Labor and material were freely given by the most public-spirited citizens; and one still among us, then about ten years old, Capt. M. F. Dickinson, remembers helping his father draw sand used in the construction of the first building. Mr. Zachariah Hawley of Hadley, now living, remembers drawing stone at the same time.

One building after another has been added to Amherst College, and the funds have accumulated until the whole property amounts to more than $1,000,000. It has educated more than 2,400 men.

The Agricultural College was founded in 1867. The town contributed $50,000 after the State had located it here. Its present property and funds are valued at $500,000.

With 346 students in Amherst College, 115 in the Agricultural College, and over 500 pupils in our public schools, Amherst shows material progress in educational advantages since Josiah Pierce gave up his work in 1769.

In 1767, Simeon Smith (son of Moses Smith, tavern-keeper on the Bay-road) began teaming to Boston, being the first to drive through with a wagon, and more than a week was consumed in the trip—while now the railroad delivers to us in the morning freight that was loaded in Boston the night before, and frequent passenger trains take us to Boston or New York in a few hours with a comfort greatly in contrast with the saddle of 1739, and the teams of 1767—while the vast network of railroads, reaching throughout the land and into Canada on the north and Mexico in the far south, put us in quick and easy communication with all this vast domain, the greater portion of which, in 1739, was the home only of the Aborigines.

About the year 1815, only once a week, a man on horseback brought the mail for the entire town to Postmaster Rufus Kellogg at East Amherst, and the blowing of a horn or conch shell summoned the farmer-postmaster from the field to open the mail.

To-day eight incoming mails, and as many outgoing, are necessary to accommodate our people, while the telegraph and telephone put us in instant communication with nearly the entire civilized world.

---

*W. S. Tyler's History of Amherst College.

The letters we have read this morning were written in Boston last evening,—in Chicago yesterday, or in San Francisco only a few days ago, while any that Simeon Smith might have brought from far-away Boston, were a week old before his lumbering wagon could make the journey home.

The beautiful Village Common is one of the most notable of the signs of progress. Many here will contrast its present beauty with its unsightly appearance 30 or 40 years ago, made up as it then was of swampy ground,—frog pond, and general unevenness and signs of neglect.

Amherst has grown. Its well furnished stores and fine markets abundantly supply the ever increasing wants of its people; its two large straw-hat manufactories disburse $100,000 or more annually; and, together with its paper, lumber, carriage and other works, furnish employment to several hundred people.

Our Savings Bank, with its nearly $1,300,000 of deposits, and our National Bank, with its more than $200,000 of capital and surplus, nearly all the savings of our own people, are evidence of our progress in material things; while the nearly 900 substantial, well-kept, and tasteful homes give evidence of increased comfort and prosperity.

We should not forget, in the abundant progress of wealth and comfort, which God has thus given us, that the same sun just as brightly as now the Pelham horizon in the morning shone down from upon those Pioneers of 150 years ago, and its departing rays lighted up the rugged hills to the East just as gorgeously—but otherwise how changed! Instead of a little clearing of a few acres, a most beautiful town, and growing each year more attractive!

The Past is full of Material Progress, and are we not right in anticipating for every future anniversary occasion still greater evidence of advancement in everything that tends to make our town sought out and noted, not only for its beautiful location, surroundings and educational advantages, but also for its advancement in good morals and everything that tends to the welfare of its people!

REMINISCENCES.

PAPER

By REV. AARON M. COLTON.

Ordained June 10, 1840. Dismissed Jan. 4, 1853

The authorities here bid me use the utmost freedom in personal reminiscence. The egotism involved must be borne with.
Well remember my first journey hither; specially the ride from Palmer; the muddy roads; the shell and shackle of a coach, with more than a mild flavor of antiquity about it; harness giving out three times before we reached Belchertown; our Jonathan of a driver well equipped with straps and strings against contingencies. No "Sheridan's ride" that. Called, as by direction, on Edward Dickinson, Esq., then occupying the east part of Gen. Mack's house. After tea with him, a Mr. Luke Sweetser came with lantern and led me up through a piece of woods to his house among the trees. Sabbath morning and a nervous headache. Asked Rev. Mr. Spofford to sit with me and offer the long prayer. And what did he pray for? *One* thing, certainly : "That in the question and trial now before us, thy young servant and this people may be guided by the wisdom from above, and be led to such a conclusion as will be for the glory of God, and the interests of His kingdom." Good man, this Mr. Spofford: I forgave him, and forgive him now. But Oh! and alas! to be strung up like that to begin with.
Got through that day and evening somehow. The next morning the church and parish committees met at the office of Edward Dickinson, Esq. I was asked to be present. They had in some way rightly learned that in coming I had in mind to stay but two Sabbaths at most. Against this they strongly protested. My own mind was unalterably fixed. *Candidating!* Whereunto shall I liken it? Be-

hold and consider a fish caught with a hook, and hung up by the gills. To think of it; a man standing in a pulpit before a people, all eyes and ears eagerly intent on learning what manner of man this is, and himself, if it be so with him, saying impliedly: " Won't you, beloved, take me for your minister? Do, please." Well, some persons, strung and tuned humanly, can do some things which others can not. A public sentiment just now is worthily asking that our executions for murder be by electricity, and so be as short and painless as possible. The letter to me said, "*supply;*" and I had come with thoughts as far from candidating as I could be, and yet be here.

After nearly a two hours' talk, it was decided that I should remain and preach on the following Sabbath, and that, in the meantime, I should call on the families of the parish—the committees taking turns in leading me about. Of that week's work, Esq. Dickinson was said to have said: " That Colton is a marvel of a man—to visit two hundred families in one week, and tire out seven committee-men, and pat every woman's baby."

The two Sabbaths I have now spoken of were the first and second in March, 1840. The call came in due time. June 10th following was appointed for my ordination.

I here reach a point in personal experience memorable indeed to me. I had come to Amherst; was counseled to come by the Andover Seminary Faculty; came to a large church and parish; to a people intimately connected with a chief New England college, of which I had not been a member; came from long and close seclusion of student life; to new scenes, cares, toils, burdens. Could I prove equal to the demands? Many, my best friends, were in doubt of me. Wouldn't it have been better to begin with a less exacting charge?

Tuesday, June 9th. Came from Boston with my preacher, Rev. Wm. M. Rogers of that city. Council waiting for us at the house of Mr. Gideon Delano in Amity Street. Council organized at 2 P. M. with President Humphrey as moderator. Documents presented and approved. Then the march to the church—moderator and candidate arm in arm, and followed by a large company, representatives of the churches. Something of *form* if not of comeliness in the times of old. Large gathering in the church. Stood nearly two hours for examination. Whether I stood the examination itself, I do not say. Coming out of the church after that ordeal, I was met at the door by a Mr. Clark Green, asking me to come to his house on the evening of the next day (Ordination day), and marry his daughter. Well, well; didn't this mean business and binding?

Ordination day, Wednesday, June 10. Charming day. Great number of friends from down the River. Church filled. The *Hampshire Gazette* of the following Tuesday said: "All the parts were listened to with very unusual interest. The sermon was masterly in matter and manner. Dr. Humphrey, giving charge to the people, said: 'When your pastor comes, receive him wherever you may be. Disturb no dust; make no apologies; do not spend the first half of the visit in complaining because he doesn't come oftener, and the last half because it is so short; but make his visit so pleasant that he *can't* stay away.'"

Thus the great day and occasion—great to me.

At evening twilight I was on my way to the wedding in Mill Valley. Met Judge Dickinson in the road opposite the president's house. Saw at once from his dress and unshaven face that he had not attended my ordination. Was it come to this at my beginnings here? Deacon in the church, college educated; one of the wealthiest in the town. No matter now for the reasons, if I ever knew them, of this holding back. Enough my grateful testimony, that Judge Dickinson became in no long time, and continued to the last, to be one of my best friends and helpers.

Leaving the wedding party, I returned to the Amherst House to my room, south front, directly over the office. But there was no sleep for me that night, nor lying down. *Two such days*, with their draughts on nature, the exactions and exhaustions. The strain was nigh to breaking. Once in the night I said to myself, "This is all a dream, and I shall wake, and be relieved." But, the curtain turned aside, and, the full moon shining brightly, down there in plain sight were the signs on offices and stores. "This certainly is no dream." Then a more than half purpose to leave Amherst before morning. Knew and said, "There will be a noise over this: 'Strange freak; man called and settled, and ran away the first night.'" But then there were five reasons which might satisfy my friends—chiefly this,—that I had been unwisely counseled to come here, instead of taking one of the lighter charges that had been offered me. Then there were thoughts of dark and desperate expedients. Blessed thing that morning follows night. But *that* morning brought no relief to me. At 10 o'clock Mr. J. S. Adams called. Saw I was cast down. His gentleness of voice and ways some of you can remember. But there was as yet no casement. Providential that the weekly church prayer-meeting came that (Thursday) afternoon. Large attendance at the church. Took my place behind the communion table; invoked a blessing; read a brief Scripture. Then said, "I had always thought that, in assuming a pastoral charge, one took upon himself a great burden, but I never *felt* it as I did now." I was not able to speak further. Dea. Mack quickly rose and said: "O! our pastor mustn't think so; the burden is *mutual;* it is on us all as well as on him; and we all, pastor and people, will help each other all we can. And, best of all, God will help us, and we shall be stayed up."

Then he prayed for "our pastor," and another prayed, and another. The meeting closed. On my way to my room, at a spot between the homes of Prof. Fowler and Mrs. Moore, the terrible load rolled off suddenly and wholly; and if I ever went to my knees and thanked God for a great deliverance, I did so then. I have seen something of care, and toil, and pain. But such a horror of great darkness has so far been but *once* upon me, and I hope and pray that the same, or the like of it, may not come on me again.

Perhaps I am wrong in saying all this here and now. If so, it can be forgiven me. I have never before spoken it in public excepting once and in part—in giving the right hand to a young brother assuming a similar charge.

A year or two before I came here, the parish had voted that the pastor, Mr. Bent, receiving presents from non-parish members of the congregation, should account for the same to the parish. I had been here but a few weeks, when a handsome traveling valise was sent me. I well divined it was a *tester*—to see what the new man would do about it. I returned the gift, and with it as pleasant a letter as I knew how to write, thanking the donor for his kindness, and adding, that I could not give to the parish the present he had sent to me, and that it would not do for me to break a parish rule. To the first meeting of the parish thereafter, I sent word that the rule was embarrassing me in my parish visitation. The rule was rescinded, and then the men who had signed off returned to their place and part; and so that ripple sank from view.

Perhaps some of the ancients here can call to remembrance the old pulpit in our meeting-house in 1840. Of pine wood, narrow, doored, and achingly plain. Man up there had to look well to his elbows in essaying a gesture. High and closed against all assaults; but so were the old Bastile towers in which prisoners were immured.

In 1842 or 3 the parish obtained from Boston a new pulpit—a costly and very comely affair for those times. Then there were other fixings and furnishings. Then the grounds around the church must be graded and put in shape—a labor of days and many hands. You might have seen Lawyer Osmyn Baker, coat off, and ax in hand, pleading three hours in masterful logic for the ejectment of a stump from its ancient tenure and holding on domain of the said church aforesaid. There was admirable enterprise. The people had a mind to work.

I am not able to boast that in coming here, I found a church and parish weak, and in leaving left them strong. They were strong from the first of my knowing them, or knowing of them. Perhaps the parish has never since been stronger as to number, character, wealth, and standing of chief men. To show this to one whose memory can stretch itself to the men and things here fifty years ago, one has only to speak some of the names then found here. Deacons, Eleazer Gaylord, John Leland, John Dickinson, David Mack and Isaac Hawley; lawyers, Edward Dickinson, Osmyn Baker, Lucius Boltwood, and, a little later, Charles Delano and Samuel T. Spaulding; doctors, Sellon, Gridley, Dorrance and Cutler; merchants, Mack & Son, James Kellogg & Son, Sweetser & Cutler, Pitkin & Kellogg and Holland; Revs. Sanford and Spofford; Teacher, Nahum Gale of the Academy; Editor, J. R. Trumbull; Mr. Green and Joseph Sweetser of the Amherst Bank; Col. Warren Howland, Messrs. Fiske Cutler, Andrew Wilson, Thomas Jones, J. S. and C. Adams, S. C. Carter, Simeon Clark, Newton Fitch, Linus Green, David Parsons, Aaron Belden, Horace Smith, Martin Kellogg, Chester Kellogg, Seth Nims, Postmaster Strong; the Smiths, Bakers, Boltwoods, Kelloggs, Dexters and Williamses of Mill Valley; the Cowlses, Hawleys and Nashes of Plainville; and the names Cowls, Angier, Bangs, Ayres, Eastman and Dickinson of the North roads; these and more—for I draw from memory, and must stop somewhere.

Surely a field, this, to call for and call out the best and most that any minister could have and give.

As to those my Deacons, specially the first four; venerable men in form and aspect, all verging toward seventy years of age, crowned with hoary heads, men of affairs, and wise in counsel. Happily for us, we didn't then turn off our deacons every year or two—a practice I never believed in, and never shall.

Don't you now be too hard on a young minister if, unawares, there sometimes stole into his heart a timorous fragrance, just a bit of sly elation, at seeing those venerable forms, his deacons, pass round with the bread and wine in the communion hour and service. We are human still—some of us are—having, I hope, a little of grace with our much of nature.

It was a point of trial in those days, that this church and parish had no parsonage, no chapel or vestry. Our evening meetings were held in the Academy building, then in care of a student, aided and aiding himself in preparation for the ministry—the late Rev. Dr. Isaac Bliss of Constantinople. Happily for pastor and people, and in the behoof of all that is fair and right, those aching voids here have been filled, to the joy and praise of many.

And then as to the old meeting-house on the hill, whither the tribes went up. Homely in outward looks, doubtless, but handsome within—so we felt. The Lord was there in the beauty of his holiness; and his presence will make any place beautiful. As for the rest, I for one, was never kept awake o'nights. Rowland Hill once said: " Never mind for the hive; give us the bees." I give joy to my successors, my brethren beloved, that they have the hive, and the bees, and the handsomeness all through and around.

In those times of old there were here a few spots a little steep and rough in a minister's work. One was, his having to preach two sermons on Fast Days. Another was, his having to preach two sermons on Communion Days, administer the Sacrament at noon, and —a last straw—attend a prayer meeting in the evening. And the tired toiler betook himself, as best he could, to the soothing persuasion, " mollifying ointment," that he was obeying the Apostle's injunctions: " make FULL proof of your ministry," and " endure hardness as a good soldier of Jesus Christ." Once the suggestion was made by some one to have the communion service occupy the afternoon. But there was opposition to this, and the matter was dropped. It was the " *custom* " here, and in some places hereabouts, and custom, you know, is law, and law is law, and what is not law is something else. " Innocuous desuetude " hadn't arrived in these parts. A somewhat of the strict and rigid, you will say, in these things of the olden time. Perhaps so; but possibly the pendulum is now swinging to the other and not better extreme.

It is not my part to-day to give the history of this church. Another has done this. But I may, I think, and should, refer in a word to the *revivals* here in 1841, '45 and '50. This last was a work of marked depth and power. The incidents and influences leading to it are quite instructive. Early in January of this year (1850) the prayer meetings were notably fuller and more solemn. A cloud of mercy seemed to hang over us, and ready to drop down fatness. Days and weeks passed, but no conversions. What was the hindrance? Once and again the church standing committee—the Deacons—met in the pastor's study to talk and pray over this question. Oppressing fear was felt, lest our dawn should shut down in darkness. The *trouble*, we came at length to believe, was in the rum places in the village, with fires of hell in full blast. What could be done? My counselors did wisely in advising prudence, for we were told the rum men were desperate. Kind words had been used, but availed nothing. You can imagine a pastor's anxieties in such an emergency. March meeting was close by. I drew up two articles, and obtained five signatures, asking for their insertion in the warrant: First, to see if it be the wish of the town of Amherst that places be kept open here for the sale of intoxicating drinks in violation of law; and second, to see if the town will authorize and instruct their selectmen to *close* such places, if such there be in the town. (I quote from memory and for substance.) I went to Lieutenant Dickinson of the South parish, and Judge Conkey of the East, and Daniel Dickinson of the North, and President Hitchcock of the College. They all promised to give a helping word—Dr. Hitchcock to speak last. The meeting came. Sweetser's hall was crowded to the stairs. There was much excitement. A man from South Amherst moved that the articles be dismissed. This was voted down. Then the main question, and now the speaking, as pre-arranged—Dr. Hitchcock closing,—and a more affecting and effective appeal than his I have never heard. He said in substance: "The people of Amherst are aware that I have not been in the habit of meddling in the affairs of the town. I feel that the interests of myself and my family are safe in the care of the town, and I am confident that the good people here who have done so nobly for the College will not allow the Institution to suffer injuries from evil causes among us;" and then, with an emphasis that fairly choked his utterance, he added: "*But it were better that the college should go down, than that young men should come here to be ruined by drink places among us.*" Then the voting—400 hands shot up for abating the nuisances—so it was said. Contrary minds—just *one* hand, and one only and alone. The next morning at ten o'clock the selectmen went to these rum resorts and shut them up.

Then the heavens gave rain—blessed showers, and there was a great refreshing. That revival work continued till late in summer. More than 150 professed hope in Christ; 68 persons joined this church on profession, on one day—Aug. 11. Others came later; some joined elsewhere.

I cannot let this opportunity pass, without expressing my very great obligations to the Faculty of Amherst College, for their unvarying courtesy and kindness to me from first to last of my labors here. Fathers and brothers could not have been more friendly and helpful. One member of that Faculty, Professor William S. Tyler, revered and beloved, is still spared to us; and my best impulses prompt me to say, that a kinder heart than his I have never found.

It has providentially been my favored lot to minister to *two* peoples, and *only* two, in the gospel of Christ. They were and are good peoples. I never desired any better peoples. I never sought nor desired any other peoples. These have I loved, and I love them still. If any one be curious to ask, which of my two peoples I love most and best, my instant answer is—*both*.

PAPER

By REV. EDWARD S. DWIGHT, D. D.

(Became Acting Pastor Aug. 21, 1853. Installed July 19, 1854. Dismissed Aug. 28, 1860.)

I was invited to take the pastoral charge of this church, to occupy, if not to fill, the vacancy left by my loved and now venerable brother, the Rev. Aaron M. Colton, in the early summer of 1853; and having conditionally accepted the invitation, entered on my official duty on the 21st of Aug. Domestic considerations seemed to me to render my immediate installation unadvisable, and it was postponed for a time.

The Amherst of that day wore a very different aspect from that which it now presents. The natural land-marks were indeed all in view. The country around was as beautiful then as now. But the town itself, the buildings, public and private, the streets, the open grounds, were only such as were at that time to be everywhere seen in our country towns. There were numerous neat and substantial homes, of the plain style of a former generation; but not one tasteful edifice—such as we see now on every side—from the factory-like range of barracks on College Hill to Mt. Pleasant on the North. A short strip of pavement lay on the two sides of the square corner near the hotel, where the business of the population centered; and elsewhere were simple gravel walks, more or less carefully kept. The common was a rudely fenced field, wholly uninviting to the eye; while the streets were too apt to be littered with loose papers and other rubbish. (I heard an eminent gentleman, who lived among you a few years ago, and who had traveled far and wide,—the late Admiral Green,—pronounce Amherst the most attractive town in every respect that he had ever known. He would hardly have said so then.)

I, of course, inherited my brother Colton's church and society. The church had its full quota of four deacons, Messrs. Luke Sweetser, Simeon Clark, Moses B. Green and Josiah Ayres. The two last named had been recently chosen, and it was one of my early duties to set them formally apart to their office with public prayer. It was my happiness to be associated with them officially through my whole pastorate, and to find in them always judicious counsellors and cordial friends. With Mr. Sweetser, the upright merchant, the sagacious citizen, the earnest christian, my relations were during that period and to the end of his life, of an especially warm and cordial nature; and in his house I found a home, whenever duty brought me here in later years. The junior deacon, Mr. Ayres, the popular janitor of the college, died at the very close of my ministry, and almost my last public duty here was to conduct the service at his funeral.

The church membership fell somewhat short of 300. Among its more prominent members were, Gen. Mack, the living presentment—as it seemed to me—of a Puritan of the olden time, with integrity and godly-fear stamped on every feature, who to my regret survived only a year or two after I came to know him; Dea. Leland, already well advanced in years, and approaching the end of his useful life; Mr. Edward Dickinson, the strong, high-minded, public-spirited citizen, whom all honored and trusted; Mr. Lucius Boltwood, conservative, clear in his convictions and true to them, candidate of the Free-soil party for years for the Governor's chair, which he would have filled more worthily than some who have reached it: Mr. John S. Adams, the intelligent, kindly book-seller, whose store was the head-quarters of the literary society of the town; and David Parsons, (as everybody called him, son of the second pastor of the church, quiet, shrewd, ingenious, whose bright wit made his carpenter's shop a place of hardly less attraction in another way:—not to add to these names those of the "honorable women," whose good sense and christian worth adorned their respective homes.

The old customs had not all passed away. It was one of the odd experiences of my first years in Amherst, to see our venerable brother, Mr. Carter, (whom you laid away to his rest only a few weeks ago), rise in his pew under the south gallery, in his almost life-long capacity as town clerk, just after the afternoon congregation had assembled, and before the worship began, and read in not too loud a voice "the intentions of marriage" of parties contemplating forming that relation, while all ears were intent to catch their names. It was not very long, however, before this custom was superseded by the more agreeable usage that now prevails.

Among the earlier changes that speedily followed (I will not say, that were owing to) my coming, was that which was made in the music of our public worship. I found a choir of ten or fifteen singers in the gallery under the leadership of Dr. Woodford, with an orchestra consisting of a bass-viol, a violin and a flute: the latter played, I think, by Mr. George Cutler: I do not remember who played the former. I am not competent to criticize the merits of their music. But the congregation were growing ambitious of something more modern; and a move was soon made, and successfully carried out, to procure an excellent organ,—as it was then regarded,—at what was for those days a very heavy expense. Its introduction gave universal and very great satisfaction.

The cause that occasioned the delay of my final settlement not continuing, I was installed as pastor on July 19, 1854, by a council of which Dr. Woodbridge, of Hadley, was the moderator. From the experiences of other candidates before other councils at the Doctor's hands, I had fully expected to have my theological beliefs thoroughly overhauled, and perhaps sharply antagonized, by him, in his character as the famous local champion of rigid orthodoxy. But to my astonishment he skillfully evaded all disputed points, and I passed the examination without a single "condition." I had asked my honored relative and old college tutor, President Woolsey, of Yale, to preach the sermon, and he had promised to do so, but found himself—as the time drew near—unable to be absent from his college duties. Thereupon, I had recourse to Dr. Leonard Bacon, of New Haven, (so well known through New England), who kindly consented to render the service. Dr. Cleveland, then of the First church in Northampton, was on the council, but had no part in its public exercises assigned him. He therefore asked to be excused from further attendance, giving as his reason that "it was unnecessary, as he knew that the *bacon* that would be furnished was always *well cooked.*" A smile of amusement at the rather rude jest lighted up the grave faces around, all save Dr. Bacon's own, who sat with countenance as grim and utterly unconscious, as though no such person as Dr. Cleveland were on the planet.

I was settled on a salary of $900, a sum that meant more then than it does now,—determined on, as I was told, as being what the college Professors were then receiving. Those gentlemen—good and worthy men that they were—had some of them been brought into very close quarters indeed, not many years before; and counted themselves happy when their compensation reached the amount I have named. Unfortunately for me, the ideas of the congregation as to what a minister was worth, did not advance as fast as the estimate the trustees of the college put on the services of its instructors; and these gentlemen consequently grew rich more rapidly than I did!

It was not very long after this, that the society took another important step forward, in building its very neat and comfortable vestry west of the church for its business and social meetings. Previously, the Sunday evening worship and the weekly prayer-meetings were held (as my brother Colton no doubt well remembers) in the basement of the church itself, a most uninviting room, low-ceiled and dark and half-subterranean; so that our removal into the light, airy, well ventilated and comfortably seated new edifice, was an occasion (to those, at least, who *attended* the meetings) of hearty mutual congratulation. It was as great an improvement on anything we had known before, as the present beautiful room in which you are now privileged to hold such services is upon the one we valued so highly.

The year 1857 will be well remembered by our elder citizens, as one of national distress from the depression of business. That period of great outward disaster was followed in '58, not altogether strangely, by a correspondingly wide-spread awaking of earnest religious feeling, pervading the churches with great power. In this healthy spiritual movement we were, in the mercy of God, permitted to share freely; and the happy result was a numerous ingathering of converts, young and old, into our fellowship, adding in every respect to the church's strength. A consequence, not at the time anticipated, followed not long after. Among the new candidates for church-membership were many, to whom the phraseology of our confession of faith—theological, antiquated, clumsily expressed—was hardly intelligible; and there arose (I scarcely recall now how or with whom it originated) an inquiry whether it were not a suitable time to *recast* both creed and confession, and, without changing their doctrinal significance, to bring them into a more easily understood and more useful form. The question was then with us a novel one. The proposal naturally met with strong opposition from some of our more conservative members, attached to the creed (as it stood *written on the fly-leaf at the end of the pulpit hymn book*) because it was old, and they deemed any meddling with its time-honored terms, a crime little less heinous than sacrilege. The discussion that ensued at times grew warm, and seemed even to threaten serious division in the church. But the reasonableness of the proposed changes,— which were not violent or fundamental,— by degrees commended itself to the great majority of the members, and the minority had the good sense and good feeling to waive their objections. The proposed alterations were made, and peace was preserved. In a later pastorate still more extensive changes of the same general nature were made, on which, it seems to me, you are to be congratulated.

I have found among my papers the records of the *charities* of the church, for four years of my ministry, from '54 to '57 inclusive; and it surprises me to read for those years respectively the footings of $1,072, $988, $1,001 and $810; which impress me now as showing— for those times—a very creditable spirit of christian liberality.

The relations of my ministry with the gentlemen of the college faculty, beginning with the eminent but very modest President Hitchcock, and afterwards much more intimately with President Stearns and the different professors, were always of the most friendly and pleasant kind. Never did they refuse me any aid which—as was not seldom the case—I had occasion to request.

Family considerations again seemed to render it my duty, in 1860, to seek a more genial climate for my household, and I offered my resignation of the pastorate in that year, to take effect on the 10th of August, seven years from the time of my entering on its duties. The church and society granted my request for release, with kind expressions of regret and good-will.

May I add (in closing these imperfect recollections of a pleasant ministry long past by, the survivors of which have already come to be comparatively few in number), as an expression of my personal interest in the prosperity of this now historical church, a single stanza from a hymn we used to sing in the old days of "Watts and Select," but which is now seldom if ever heard?—

> "May peace attend thy gate,
> And joy within thee wait,
>   To bless the soul of every guest!
> The man that seeks thy peace,
> And wishes thine increase,
>   A thousand blessings on him rest!"

NOTE. On page 80, nineteenth line from the bottom read Dr. Woodman.

LETTER

BY REV. HENRY L. HUBBELL, D. D.

Ordained April 24, 1861. Dismissed April 4, 1865.

Unable to be present, to my great disappointment, at the interesting exercises of your one hundred and fiftieth anniversary, I am requested to speak by letter. Though pressed with other duties, my love to the church is such I cannot refuse.

It is a rare privilege, granted to but a few, to start a stream of organized influence and activity perpetuating itself in a community for one hundred and fifty years. This honor belongs to the founders of this church which has become the mother of other churches, and a College, shedding its light even into foreign lands.

Next to starting, is the honor of continuing, directing and enlarging such organized influence and activity in the service of Christ and his civilization. It is this, my friends, which gives us all an opportunity to honor the founders and join in the celebration of to-day. Each of us entered into the life and work of this church in a way peculiar to himself and each has done his own individual work, because God never duplicates his servants or their services.

My own entrance and continuance in the life and activity of the church, has for me some points of very special interest. Here I began my ministry. I came fresh from Andover Theological Seminary, counseled to come by Prof. Phelps, also by Prof. Park, who had lived among you while he was Professor in the College and commended the church very highly.

By this church I was ordained to the Christian ministry and installed your pastor, April 24, 1861. Prof. Phelps preached the sermon. The examination before the Council, except one point, I remember dimly, but most impressively the ordination with " the laying on of hands," enjoining on me a ministry to the Master and a service to you that, in the measure in which I sought to fulfill it, seemed to rise above my reach more and more. Here I began new experiences, new relations, new cares, new prayers, new affections for those I sought to serve, prayers and affections that abide to this day.

In this church, too, I found *one*, who, as I esteemed it, more than doubled my services to you and more than doubled my life in all that made life worth living.

Besides these new things which never become old, we began our common service to the Master, at a new epoch of our country's history and under very distracting conditions for purely spiritual work.

Ten days before I came, President Lincoln issued his Proclamation for 75,000 men. Had not Seminary advice checked me, I should have asked of you release, and joined the army. But I came. I found the air filled with the sounds of war and the rumors of war. The recruiting office was in the street. In a short time, sons of the Faculty, members of my congregation and one of the Professors had enlisted. The whole community was stirred with the preparations and the excitements of the approaching conflict. After Bull Run we knew not how long it would last. We dreaded what we feared. At first, not all the church was in sympathy with the uprising of the people. The majority were, and ere long we were substantially one in the great struggle for national life and liberty. We sent out our quota. We saw them, with others, march proudly away under the dear old flag, keeping time to the inspiring music of war. In imagination we went with them, through the streets of the great cities, through the towns and open country, into camps at the front. By

Sanitary and Christian Commission services, by speeches and votes, by sympathies and prayers, we stood by them when on guard in the cold storm and beneath clear, sunny skies. on the long, weary march and the bloody field of battle, in hospitals of pain and prisons of "hatred and famine" and when, between the contending lines, life was slowly ebbing away,—but who can count up their sufferings! In yonder cemetery lies the precious dust of some: the dust of others, equally precious, sleeps in unknown graves in the land they made free.

In the summer heat of 1864 I had the privilege of being your representative to our brave men at the front. In the preaching-places, by the bedside of the sick, the wounded and the dying, I told these men who sent me, and endeavored to cheer and comfort them by pointing them to Jesus Christ. In due time the struggle was over. Law and liberty triumphed.

Though the period for this struggle was not the best for promoting revivals or proposing church improvements or new lines of church work, yet, during it, God blessed us with an increase of Spiritual life with frequent accessions and one or two special refreshings among the young, whose lives and services are to-day blessing this and other churches. I cannot but refer to some, conspicuous in their influence, while I was pastor, who have preceded us into the Silent Land. There were Deacon Sweetser and Edward Dickinson, Esq., each in their way leaders, good men and true. Lucius Boltwood, Deacon Green, Mr. Carter, Mr. Sidney Adams, and other prominent men come before my mind as worthy of special mention for what they were and did.

There were also women in this church and congregation whose faithful services have earned them a good degree and an honorable mention in the records of this church; such as Mrs. Mack, Mrs. William Cutler, Miss Esther Cutler and many others.

In many ways the life of the College touches and advantages the life of the church. Perhaps, to no one in the church is the College of more profit and pleasure than to the pastor. He feels the impulse of its intellectual and spiritual activity. I am sure I felt it and to your advantage. The College Professors never failed to help when asked. There were two to whom I felt specially indebted and of whom I asked help, perhaps oftener than others, because of our personal relations. One was Prof. Crowell, now standing in the front rank of scholars and teachers, the other was Prof. Seelye, now the distinguished President of the College, than whom no man can be a truer friend. I can bear personal testimony that both Pres. Stearns and Pres. Seelye felt a genuine interest in the prosperity of our church. One day, Prof. S. said to me that he looked on our church as the mother of the College, and he felt as he spoke. Fortunate has our church been in the friends and influences immediately about it.

Good as is your past, your future may be better. God's work is growing larger, year by year, and His grace is sufficient for every demand. May it be the privilege of yourselves and those who come after you to do that enlarging work and to be filled with that ever enlarging grace, till He comes. I can ask for the church no greater success nor for its workers any greater reward.

Lake Charles, La., Nov. 27, 1889.

ADDRESS

By REV. JONATHAN L. JENKINS, D.D.

Became Acting Pastor Feb. 17, 1867, Installed Sept. 24, 1868, Dismissed Feb. 5, 1877.

(An incomplete report, but substance of the thought.)

One good thing about the memory is that it does not remember. It seems to be controlled by natural selection. It retains what it likes. It ejects as well as keeps. This prerogative it uses in the care of what is disagreeable. This the memory shuts out. It is astonishing how soon we forget a pain, when the pain has stopped. It is because the unpleasant, the painful drops out of remembrance that the past wins a glory from being far.

It must be that during my life of ten years here disagreeable things happened. It is even possible that I myself did not please everybody. And it is quite certain everybody didn't always do what pleased me. What may have been does not now concern us. Our concern is with what is remembered. And the memory of my life here is the memory of a long, pleasant day with bright skies overhead and its hours filled up with delightful companionships.

Occasions like the present do more than give opportunity for indulgence in personal reminiscences. They should bring to mind the excellent work done in the past by the old historic churches of New England. I am a high church man, a high New England church man. The historic New England church is not an institution to be ashamed of. Its works win it praise. It was by its churches that New England was made what it is. It is to be kept true to itself by its churches, and by the churches which are successors of the churches originally planted in New England. The ideas embodied in and promulgated by those churches are neither obsolete nor useless now. They seem the very ideas needed in society. The old doctrine that men can govern themselves without interference from without, is a doctrine that can be insisted upon with profit now. So is the old doctrine that religion is not ceremony or spectacle, but a personal experience, one that the world has not yet outgrown. Nor again is it wholly unnecessary to insist that religion is of the understanding even more than of the sensibilities. There is work for the old historic churches of New England. That mission is not yet accomplished. Occasions like this are valuable that they make distinct the work to be done, and unite faith in agencies suited to accomplish the work. Be persuaded then, friends, to identify yourselves more and more closely with the veritable church, let it in each generation reveal its strength, and in each generation more perfectly do the work given it to do.

LETTER

By REV. F. F. EMERSON

Installed 1879. Dismissed 1883.

To the First Church and Society, Amherst, Mass.:— Dear Christian Friends:

It is with the most sincere regret, and a feeling of disappointment which I am unable to express, that on account of unexpected duties which I do not feel at liberty to put aside, I find myself unable to be present with you to participate in the festivities of your one hundred and fiftieth anniversary. As I cannot see you face to face and speak what is in my heart to say, I must fall back upon the poor alternative of sending you a few words of regret and giving a few, out of many reasons, why Amherst will be to me one of the most interesting places in the world, and why I still love the dear old church which for four years I was permitted to serve. It is nearly seven years since I was dismissed from the Amherst pastorate, but these years have fled so quickly and my mind has been so absorbed in my labor here, that it seems but a little while since I left you, and should I rise in the familiar pulpit on Thursday evening, it would be the most natural thing in the world to give out a text and go ahead with the sermon.

But I know that a different task would await me, — a task which I would gladly have fulfilled to the best of my ability, had I been permitted to be with you.

Amherst will always be of interest to me because it was there that I awoke to my Congregational consciousness; for I suppose I was always a Congregationalist, only I did not discover it till I was about forty years of age. The earliest colonial Emerson was a Puritan minister of "The Standing Order" settled in Mendon in 1632. Since his day there have been many Emersons in the Congregational pulpit. I suppose it was in the blood. For some unaccountable reason my father became a Baptist. It was, however, only a temporary aberration of the Emersonian mind; for though I was born in a Baptist family and rocked in a Baptist cradle, educated in Baptist schools and graduated from a Baptist college and seminary, and a preacher for some twelve years in Baptist pulpits, yet, as chickens hatched under the motherly protection of a duck will not take to the water, so the natural aversion of my earlier ancestors to that liquid element finally asserted itself;—I pecked my way out of the hard shell of Baptist logic and stood at last a full-feathered Congregational chick. And it was in Amherst that with wide-open eyes I looked forth upon my new world of Congregational liberty. It was a triumph of heredity over environment.

It was in Amherst, too, that I came under the altogether quickening and healthful influence of a New England College town. I was admitted to many pleasant relationships with men of learning, whose acquaintance and friendship was helpful and inspiring from first to last. Amherst is not of sufficient size not to feel the influence of the college in all its thought and activities of whatever kind. The colonial tradition has come down to us that a good minister of Boston in the early days went down to Marblehead to preach to the fishermen, and he told them that the main business of life was religion. An old salt in commenting on the sermon the next day, remarked in a grumbling tone, that the main business of life might be religion up in Boston—probably was—but in Marblehead it was *fishing*. The main business of Amherst is Amherst college; and I rejoice that my first work in the Congregational pastorate was in a town that is full of academic traditions and that feels the helpful influence upon its schools and churches of what may be called a collegiate atmosphere. As I think of the ministers with whom I daily associated and who were among my most lenient and appreciative hearers and cordial supporters and helpers, and of the professors, with many of whom I formed relatious which were most friendly and helpful, I look back upon my stay in Amherst as a veritable sojourn in a school of the prophets; a school in which he must be dull indeed who could not find inspiration and help to keep his working power up to concert pitch.

Then, too, I recall the fact that I found in Amherst a well organized church and parish; a people interested in their church life and work; a church and society thoroughly alive, with a commendable pride in their place of worship, and having the different departments well manned and equipped for the work which a church and parish ought to do in a community. It was in this respect that I felt that I owed much to the pastors who had gone before me, and sometimes thought within myself that they had done so much and so well for the church, that there was little for me to do in the way of organization, or the adoption of methods. I think the First church in Amherst could as well dispense with a pastor altogether as any church with which I am acquainted. It runs of itself.

And last, but not least, as a matter of interest to me, I remember Amherst as the place where I was treated a great deal better than I deserved. I shall never cease to remember with gratitude the kindness of the Amherst church to me and mine in many ways, how lenient they were towards my faults and failings, and how appreciative above that which they deserved, they were, of my pulpit ministrations.

I know you will call to mind on Thursday, as I do now, the forms and faces of those who were with us when I was your minister, but who are now gone to their reward: Dea. Sweetser, whose kindly and affable ways I shall never forget; Dea. Nash, with his sterling good sense and unaffected piety; and others whose memory is fragrant in the history of the church. There were two men, however, whose memory will ever be especially dear to me,—fathers in Israel whom I both respected and loved—Dr. Magill and Dr. Hickok. They have passed away since I left the pastorate of the church. Dr. Magill came to Newport at my installation and spoke so kindly and generously to the people concerning my character and gifts that the aim to fill out the outlines of the promises which he made for me, has been a serious and unfulfilled task to this day. His kindly and appreciative treatment of me during my pastorate will be among the pleasant memories of my life. And no man could be a warmer, truer friend than Dr. Hickok. It pained me, oftentimes, to think that the great thinker, philosopher, and preacher, was compelled to listen to my ineffectual theologizing, but he never let me know, by word or sign, that it troubled him. He was a constant encouragement and inspiration by his unwavering kindness, and ever renewed manifestation of interest and regard.

Permit me in closing to congratulate you on what I believe will be a most delightful occasion. Allow me to look back with you into the past, recalling what God has done for you from the earliest days of your history, onward to the present time, how many men and women have been trained for the better life in these long years, and what you have been permitted to do for the community where God has placed you. Permit me, also, to look with you into the future, with the full expectancy and hope that now, firmly established on so good a foundation, there yet remain greater and better things for you.

I shall never cease to be interested in all your doings, and to wish for you the highest welfare and success. As there is a period of your history which is especially sacred and dear to me, and which can never fade out of my memory, and for that reason mainly, all that pertains to you will ever be of the deepest interest to me.

You have had sunshine and shadow, joy and sorrow, intertwined all along your pathway, as all God's people do, but God has been using both, and overruling both, for your spiritual growth *as to yourselves*, and for your moral power *as to your influence in the community* where He has planted you. And so He will continue to do for you and for His people everywhere.

May God bless you: may the Holy Spirit guide you and make you perfect to do the Divine will; and may Christ, the Head of the church, who holds in His right hand the seven stars which are ministers of his churches, and who walks in the midst of the seven golden candlesticks which are the churches themselves, bless and keep and perfectly redeem you;—that "you may walk worthy of the Lord unto all pleasing, being fruitful in every good work, and increasing in the knowledge of God."

Yours in the gospel of Christ,
FORREST F. EMERSON.

ADDRESS

BY REV. E. P. BLODGETT.

Greenwich, Mass.

There is no local church which has so large a place in my heart, as this First church in Amherst, unless it be the church of which I have been the pastor more than forty-six years and whose one hundred and fiftieth anniversary, 1749—1899, will occur ten years from this date. I united with this church fifty-eight years ago, and continuously without interruption, have been a member of it, until six years ago, when I removed my relation to the church of which I had been so long pastor, the reason of which abiding here and of my subsequent removal, I need not here detail. For six years, therefore, I have been without a pastor. Previously, ten of the pastors of this church had stood in the ecclesiastical relation of pastor to me. I am one of the very few surviving who unite the present with the past, reaching back nearly seventy years. I have no records except what are written upon the tablet of memory. The old meeting-house on the hill, the religious home of the church for so many years, from the top of the old steeple to its foundation stones I remember well. In all its comeliness, or rather uncomeliness, I have a distinct recollection of it. I remember its square pews with the seats turned up on hinges during the long prayer. In one of them sat Noah Webster and his family during his residence in Amherst, while engaged in the great work of his life. The old high pulpit perched far above the heads of the hearers, with the deacons' seat in front below, and the sounding board especially, suspended from the ceiling over the head of the minister, are in vivid remembrance, and it was one of the trials of my early boyhood, lest that sounding board might fall and crush the messenger of God in the very act of delivering his message. I remember the choir opposite the pulpit in the side gallery, with Moses Dickinson as its leader, with no musical instrument attached to it except the old fashioned pitch pipe whose toot I can now almost hear. I remember the large square pews or pens in the galleries, which were such a convenient refuge for the naughty boys who afforded abundant material for the tithing man, one of whom I especially recall in the person of Col. Howland, and I remember too, when about six years old, going from the old meeting-house to the ceremony of laying the corner stone of the first building of Amherst college, in which the First church in Amherst took such a vital interest in its early struggle for existence, and once more I remember vividly the forenoon of the very day when the old steeple fell a crash to the earth, and the building was taken down to give place to a future home of the church in what is now College hall, and in after years to the astronomical observatory in the old locality.

My remembrance of Dr. Parsons is somewhat dim, and yet with great vividness I recollect the day it was announced in Amherst, that he was dead in Wethersfield, whither he had gone to visit relatives. But Daniel A. Clark rises up before me in all the impressiveness of his remarkable personality. He was an eminent preacher of great gifts as a sermonizer, graphic in style, with pith and point as all who have his sermons in print will bear witness. Royal Washburn, his successor, was a name to be revered and loved; royal not in name merely, but in nature: royal in his manhood, royal in his ministry and in all his influence as a servant of God. A saintly, Christly man, with a character as simple and unostentatious as the plain, marble slab erected to his memory, and as beautiful as the epitaph upon it,— " Saved by grace." I was one of the last group admitted to the church under his ministry and, I think, the last person baptized by him before he entered upon that eventful journey to Georgia, for his health and returning in the spring not much improved he lingered some months in the chamber of the, then, parsonage, but since occupied for many years by Mrs. Davis. One incident, during those months of decline, shows the man. Amherst college had received from the state its charter in full, after a long struggle and opposition. As a demonstration of joy it was illuminated from the top of the tower downward at every available window in south, middle and north colleges. A grand sight. Mr. Washburn was asked to be taken from his bed that he might witness it. He was carried to the window where he might have a full view. "Beautiful" he exclaims. "But I have a grander sight still. · I see the glory of God in the face of Jesus Christ'." And we do not wonder that at his funeral Prof. Fiske should take as his text. " Precious in the sight of the Lord is the death of his saints."

But I must not linger. I have known all the ministers of this church from Dr. Parsons, or Daniel A. Clark at least, to the present pastor. Some of them have gone up higher. Some of them still in active work for the Master. One in his green old age still bringing forth fruit, whose voice you had hoped to hear to-day. And then those deacons, too, Dea. Leland, the music of whose voice still lingers in mine ear. Dea. Gaylord of whom it was said, if a difficult case of discipline occurred in the church, such was his wisdom and christian sagacity combined with tenderness, it was committed especially to his care. Dea. David Mack and Dea. Zachariah Hawley, whose large and well-proportioned bodies were equaled or exceeded by their sound judgment, solid practical sense and consecrated piety. A long list I might go over, I might call the roll, good men and godly women not a few, whose very presence in the streets of Amherst, was a vindication of everything good and pure and Christly and a rebuke of everything mean and false and wicked. They believed because God had spoken. They had positive convictions and the courage of their convictions. They believed in, and held to the covenant, and that the covenant-keeping God held them. They have passed away, one after another, to the great congregation of the just; one of them within a few months, in the person of Samuel C. Carter. And may all the present membership be so loyal to their discipleship, that the church shall more and more continue to have an uplifting power in this community and in its missionary zeal be a benediction unto the ends of the earth.

LETTERS.

Given below are a few of many letters from persons who received the invitation of the Church to the celebration.

First Church Parsonage,
Hartford, Conn., Oct. 19, 1889.

MY DEAR MR. DICKERMAN :—

I have your kind letter of invitation to the one hundred and fiftieth anniversary of the organization of the First church of Christ in Amherst. I should most gladly be present on the occasion, not only because of the general interest I feel in historical anniversaries of this kind, but in especial because of the peculiar relationship which you have yourself suggested between the Amherst church and the First church of Hartford, through the medium of the Hadley church formed by the seceding members of the church of which I have the honor to be pastor. I have had occasion elsewhere quite carefully to examine the controversy which led to the secession spoken of, and to express the opinion that "spite of many irregularities and, doubtless, a good deal of ill temper on both sides, the general weight of right and justice was with the defeated and emigrating minority."

Loyal, therefore, as I am, and have reason to be, to the old church from whom this minority went away, and highly as I esteem the character of the fathers who remained and the sons who have succeeded to them, I can but have a prepossession of interest in the band which planted themselves in Hadley and their successors who laid the foundations in Amherst.

Recognizing in some sense the grandmotherly relation in an ecclesiastical way of the church of which I am pastor, to that to which you bear the like relation, let me extend in the name of the First church of Hartford, our kind congratulations on your prosperity, and our hopes for the happy and useful celebration of your anniversary.

These congratulations I would cheerfully and gladly bear in person, did not a previous engagement absolutely forbid. I trust that the presence with you of an honored member of our church, John C. Parsons, Esq., a representative of two of your early and revered pastors, will more than supply any deficiency on my part.

Yours very truly,
GEO. LEON WALKER.

Cleveland, Ohio, Nov. 4, 1889.

MR. WILLIAM W. HUNT,

My Dear Sir:—

When I wrote you some days ago, I fully intended to accept the invitation of the committee, to be present at the celebration of the one hundred and fiftieth anniversary of the First church of Christ, of Amherst, on the 7th inst. But my engagements are such, it will be impossible for me to leave Cleveland, in time to be with you, and I reluctantly send my regrets.

To me the anniversary has a peculiar interest. For nearly a period covering three generations, my grandfather and great-grandfather were pastors of this church. They were pious, influential, devoted men, and did their work well and bravely in the world. In early life I knew a distinguished lawyer of Connecticut, who knew my grandfather intimately, and he spoke of him in the highest terms for purity, dignity and genuine Christian character. His picture represents a man of unusual nobility of force and person, with a head of strongly marked intellectual power. That these two men should have successively filled the pulpit of this church for so many years, in the midst of so intelligent and educated a people as those of Amherst, is a sufficient endorsement of their fitness for their calling. I believe it was owing to the influence of my grandfather, that the academy at Amherst was founded, which afterwards became the nucleus of the present College. Trusting the anniversary will prove most interesting to all who attend it, I can only regret that the larger part of all the puritans, men and women, who upheld the banner of the cross in this church, "have fallen asleep," and their memory alone remains, a precious legacy to their descendants.

With the highest respect, I am very sincerely yours,

R. C. PARSONS.

Knoxville, Tenn., Sept. 30, 1889.

REV. G. S. DICKERMAN,

Dear Sir:

Your letter of the 24th inst. calls up both sad and pleasant reminiscences, and I wish it were possible for me to be with you on the 7th Nov., proximo. But that seems now impossible. I am sorry to say that we never had any portrait or other likeness of my father and I have no recollection of him, as I was but two years and nine months old when he died. Prof. Tyler can give you much valuable information regarding him and can probably furnish you a copy of Prof. Fiske's funeral discourse. I have some of his sermons, as also of Dr. David Parsons, and will send you one or two of each, if my brother, John H., does not anticipate me. I have been so long remote from the place of my nativity that I am somewhat like the "lost tribes," but should you fail to receive from those nearer what you need, I shall consider it a privilege to send you the little I have.

Yours very sincerely,

W. P. WASHBURN.

---

239 W. 54 St., New York, Oct. 19, 1889.

Mr. Kingsbury sends his congratulations and kind regards to the First Church of Christ in Amherst, and thanks it heartily for the invitation to be present at the one hundred and fiftieth anniversary of its organization.

Feeble health makes it impossible for him to attend the exercises, which he knows will be so full of interest. He is often touched and gratified by word which comes to him from time to time, showing him that his son's pastorate, though so short, is still held in affectionate remembrance, and his work while in Amherst not forgotten.

With best wishes for the continued success of the church, in which Miss Kingsbury joins, and adds her regrets to those of her father that she is unable to be present on Nov. 7,

Sincerely yours,

O. R. KINGSBURY, (per H. L. K.)

Seneca Falls, N. Y., Oct. 22, 1889.

COMMITTEE OF INVITATION FIRST CHURCH OF CHRIST, AMHERST, MASS.
Dear Brethren :—

I greatly regret that I cannot have the pleasure and privilege of being present at the coming anniversary of your church's organization.

I have reason for special interest in this event. My grandfather, Rev. Josiah Bent, having died fifty years ago, while pastor of your church, and this summer his widow, after a half century of suffering, and triumphant witnessing to the sustaining power of the faith, passed to her reward and rest. All these years she retained her membership with you, and all these years, may I say, she was an active member in the truest sense.

During a part of my college course I had the privilege of worshipping in this, the church of my parents and grandparents, and now join with the many who pray for an especial blessing upon church and people.

Very sincerely yours,
EDWIN H. DICKINSON.

Ottawa, Kansas, Oct. 21, 1889.

MR WM. W. HUNT:

With deep emotion I acknowledge the cordial invitation to be present at the one hundred and fiftieth anniversary of the First church to be celebrated November seventh. Most gladly would I be with you to meet the dear friends of the Church of Christ and many others whose familiar faces and friendly greetings are fresh in my mind as I am now writing. The dearest friend, aside from my own family, was Mrs. Lucius Boltwood. A true and loving sister has been called to the mansion on high. She has written me once in two weeks since her son was taken from her. But I only intended to reply to the kind invitation to myself and children. Circumstances, I fear, will not admit of any of us being present. In imagination I see the familiar faces and hear the pleasant voices of beloved pastors and people. I have fresh in mind the pastors Rev. David Parsons, D.D., Rev. Daniel A. Clark, Rev. Royal Washburn, Rev. Matthew T. Adams, Rev. Josiah Bent, Rev. Aaron M. Colton, Rev. Mr. Hubbell, Rev. J. L. Jenkins and Rev. Mr. Kingsbury. I remember Rev. David Parsons in the pulpit with powdered wig, the sounding-board over head and the deaf man standing up at his side, leaning on the pulpit, looking anxiously to bear all he said. But to Mr. Colton and Mr. Jenkins I seem to feel bound more closely, for through sorrow and great affliction they were more with us. Rev. Mr. Dwight I have in fond remembrance. I loved pastors and people. Many I have been with in joy and in sorrow.

"Blest be the tie that binds
Our hearts in Christian love."

If Mrs. Boltwood were living how gladly would she open her beautiful home and welcome ministers and people! How much Mr. Carter, Deacon Clark, Mr. Zebina Montague, Deacon Sweetser, and too many to mention, would have enjoyed the meeting! You know not how much I have longed to take by the hand my old friends in Amherst. Many thanks to the Committee for remembering me and my family in our Kansas home.

Yours with kind remembrance.

ELECTA S. BOLTWOOD.

Vacaville, Cal., Oct. 13, 1889.

DEAR FRIEND:

Yours of the seventh inst., covering the invitation card to the Church's one hundred and fiftieth anniversary, came to hand to-day. I had noticed with interest the allusions in the *Record* to this event, so full of interest to all who love the old First church, and while it will be impossible for us to be with you in person we shall certainly be with you in spirit, and in thoughts on that day. I recall in childhood the earnest preaching of Mr. Colton, in boyhood the scholarly, cogent sermons of Mr. Dwight under whose ministry I was led to see and confess my need of Christ as my Saviour :—in young manhood I was welcomed to membership in the church by Mr. Hubbell, who gave his earliest and most faithful labors to the church as its pastor. During his ministry my children (now living) were baptised, thus securing a place in that household of faith. And of what Mr. Jenkins did for us as individual Christians, and for the church in its material prosperity, you and I know too well here to recount. Let the recollection of those memorable days and months when the new church was being built,—of the noble men who labored and gave for it, as *such* men only could, yes, let the magnificent edifice itself testify, as it shall in the ages to come. And then followed the brief but beautiful work of the Sainted Kingsbury, whom God sent here to gather our children into the fold, before God took him; and then how were we held and swayed by the masterful sermons of Emerson, and while we were but just coming under the pastorate of Mr. Dickerman our connection with the church was severed but our interest in the church has not and never can be severed. * * * * Please give kindest regards to all friends.

Yours as of old,
Geo. W. Allen.

HYMN.   Tune "Pleyel's Hymn."   Composed by Dr. V. W. Leach.

Hail Jehovah! God our King!
Loud hosannas let us raise
And to Thee glad tributes bring
On this day of joy and praise.

Tender mem'ries strike the chord,
Present blessings swell the song,
Coming ages praise the Lord
And the chorus thus prolong.

Generations gone to rest
Toiled and prayed and passed away.
We in them so richly blessed
Magnify their lives to-day.

Guide us Lord, and lead us still
In the way Thy feet have trod.
May we live to do Thy will.
Pressing on to Heaven and God.

OLD DOCUMENTS

Shown at the Anniversary.

ONE OF THE FIRST DEEDS.

[The homestead of Dr. Nathaniel Smith passed to his daughter Rebecca who married Jonathan Smith, and thence to their daughter Jerusha who married Col. Elijah Dickinson. The land given by Col. Dickinson for the college was a part of this estate.]

To all People to whom these Presents shall Come Greeting. Know ye that I Ichabod Smith of Hadley In the County of Hampshire In the Province of the masechuset Bay In New England have of my own free will and In consideration of the Paternal Love and affection which I have and Doe bare unto my Dutifull and Loving Son nathaniell Smith of Hadley affore said and as Seventy Pounds Portion out of my Estate: Have Given Granted Bargened & Bequethed fully and absolutely given and Pased over unto him my said son nathaniell Smith his Heirs Exed; adminds & assigns as a Good Estate of Inheretence In fee simple: a sartain Parsell of Land Lying in the Second Devesion of out Land within the Bounds of the township of Hadley afforesaid: viz. one half of that Lot Laid out & Recorded to me the said Ichabod Smith: the south side of said Lot and In bredth nineteen Rods containing twenty Eight acres and one half of an acre: and is Bounded north on part of the same Lot given to my son aron and south on the Lot that was m^r Gorge Stillmous: East and west on a high way or street: and also two peesis out of that Lot which was Laid ont to m^r Gorge Stillmon viz. twelve acres on the north side of said Lot In bredth Eight Rods and Bounded south on part of the same Lot given to my son aron and north on Land given to him my said son nath^ll as above said: East and west on a high way or street: and twenty nine acres and a half on the south side of Said Lot In bredth nineteen Rods and a half: Bounded north on post of the same Lot (given to my son aron): and south on a high way: and East and west on a high way or street be the said Land more or less: To have to hold Posses and Injoy to himself his Heirs Exed: adminds & assigns for Ever: with all the Rights Profits Benefits appurtenances and Preveledis thereto belonging: and I the said Icabod Smith for my self & Heirs &c. Doe Covenant and agree with my Son nathrd affore said his Heirs: &c. that I have full & Lawfull power to Give & Grant the same as affore said: and that the same is free & Clere from all former Gifts. Grants Sales Judgments Executions and Incumbrancis, and that for Ever here after I will stand to defend him my said son nath^d and his

Heirs &c. In the quiet & peasable Possession of the above graned premises against the Lawfull Demands of all Persons whatsoever: In witness of all which I set to my hand & seal this 12 Day of Decr 1730, In the third year of gorge ye Second King &c.

Signed Sealed and Delivered
In Presents and witness of

Ichabode Smith

Hamp^{sher}. Ss Decr 12th 1730.
Then m^r Ichabod Smith
before me the Subscriber
acknowledges this
Instrument to be his act
and Deed
Elea^r Porter Juste peace

Eleaz Porter
Sarah Porter
Johanah B Barnard
her mark

Rec^d & Recorded Decr the: 14th: 1730: In the records of the County of Hampshire: book N: E: Page: 501:—:

John Pynchon Reg^t

A CALL.

TO MR. DAVID PARSONS JUN.

HADLEY THIRD* PRECINCT

To Mr. David Parsons Junr at present Improved in the work of the Ministry in North Hampton Village.

The Inhabitants of this Preceinct att a Meeting held by them Janewa^y ye 10: 173$\frac{8}{7}$ agreed to give you a Call to Settle among us as oure Gospel Minister and for youre Encouragement to accept oure Request we have passed ye following Votes

For Settelment

Voted 1: two Lots of Land Lying in the Second and third Devesion of Lands granted by the Town of Hadley for the Settling of a Gospel Minister in this preceinct.

    2. To Build a Dweeling House so far as follows: to set up a frame forty foots in leuth: twenty one foots in breth two Story in heith also to Cover said House ye Roof with Sprice Shingles: ye body w quarter boards: and Build ye Chimney and Celler and also to set up a Cithing: and Cover it as ye grate House and also to build ye Chimney to s^d Cithing.

*In 1753 South Hadley was incorporated as a District, and Amherst became the second Preeinct of Hadley till 1759 when it also was made a District.

For Sallery
  Voted 1 to give one hundred pounds the first yeare in Province Bills as it is now vallied by the ounce in Silver—also to add yearly as heads and Estates shall Increas in this preceinct the same upon the pound as it amounts in Raising ye first hundred: yearly untill it amounts to one Hundred and sixty
  2 to provide his fire wood yearly
They further Required us the Subscribers to Present this theire Request to you with the Encouragement annexed: withal to Signify the unanimity of the people in their Choice and Request
We therefore as a committee in the behalf of the Preceinct Intreat you to take the matter in Consideration and as soone as youre Circumstances will allow Return us youre Answer.
(Added in different ink.)
Voted that they will allow mr Dickinson forty shillings for his preaching with us one day and half some time sinse

John Nash Jn   ) Commity in
Ebnz Dickinson } the behalf of
Richard Cnauncey) the Preceinct

Hadley third preceinct Janewʳ 10. 173$\frac{7}{8}$

at a preceinct Meeting
  Voted 1 yᵗ Each head and team shall go one day in a yeare to get his firewood during ye time of his Ministry in sᵈ preceinct
  Voted 2 to give Mr. Benjamin Dickinson forty shillings for preaching in this preceinct in time past

attested Ebnz Dickinson { moderator

To the Inhabitants of the 2ᵈ Precinct in Hadly at their Precinct meeting on Decemᵇʳ 13ᵗʰ : 1754.

Beloved:
As I am Informed you are convened upon the Annual Buisness: of Passing Precinct Debts I take the freedom again to ask for an addition to my Salary the Present year:—your kindness to my Request; the former year, I cant but Remember with Grattitude to Providence & you: without which I dont see how I could have carried it thro the year without Distressing myself & Damaging others: The great unanimity with which your kindness was done rendered it to me more especially agreeable & encourages me to ask you again for help:—To enter into a Detail of my necessities; would be as uncomfortable I Believe to you to hear as me to tell:—Let it suffice only to put you in mind, that my salary is very small; my Debts are large; my charges are very Considerable and Encreasing.
I Hope what may be done will be done with the like unanimity & good affection as heretofore which I am sure will be very much to the Satisfaction
of your obliged and
Affectionate Pastor
David Parsons.

The Precinct Records for December 13, 1754 contain the following clause.

" Voted 1 to add to the Rev'd Mr. David Parsons Sollary for this yeare ninty two pound teen shillings old tennor."

APPENDIX TO HISTORICAL ADDRESS.

A.

ANCESTRY AND FAMILIES OF THE FOUNDERS.

The following tables have been prepared to show with greater clearness whence the founders of Amherst came and how their families were interrelated. The names of the sixteen who became members of the Church at its organization and of the twenty-eight who united with them on the following January are printed in SMALL CAPITALS. The columns are so arranged that the names in each column, except the last, are of children whose parents' names are immediately to the right —the father's above and the mother's beneath, united by a brace. The last column to the right is, for the most part, of the early colonists who came from England and the place of settlement is indicated by the abbreviation. Often, however, these persons had been in different colonies. Most of them had been at first in some one of the settlements in Eastern Massachusetts, and had gone thence to other places, in a few instances to a number of places, one after the other. In such cases only one colony is named and preference is given to towns of the Hartford group.

The Amherst names on pages 105–109 are of those who came first to this Precinct. These are from Hadley and Hatfield, and their ancestors, except the Chaunceys, were mostly from Hartford and vicinity. On pages 110–111 are the names of several, including the Rev. David Parsons, who came after the settlement had become established, but was yet in its beginnings. Part of these were from other towns than Hadley and Hatfield. Mr. Parsons was from Leicester, Simeon Strong, Esq., Dea. Edwards and Dea. Clarke from Northampton, Dea. Smith from Longmeadow; and Dea. Coleman, though of Hatfield himself, had a wife from New Haven of that sterling family whence came Dr. Lyman Beecher. It will be seen that these last had more widely extended family connections, and this, no doubt, brought the community into broader associations and a more expansive life.

Names in the first column on the left are of children of the founders, the figures attached showing years of births. Dates used in the tables are only of years and in a few cases the date is only probable. The space does not allow more particulars. When the line of a family has been once given it is not repeated but referred to with "See above" or "See p."

A few names of the earliest settlers in Amherst will not be found in the tables. These are of persons concerning whom the records are scanty, and none of them had families in Amherst, so far as we know.

Philip Mattoon. p. 105 was a soldier who came with Capt. Wm. Turner from Eastern Massachusetts, having been received by him with others from Capt's Wadsworth and Reynolds at Marlboro. He settled in Deerfield and died there. His previous history is not known. The name "Philippe Maton" is given however among the immigrants, "Walloons and French," from England to Virginia in 1621; and Virginia was then understood to include New England. This Philippe Maton had a wife and five children, one of whom may have been the Philip of Deerfield.

Joseph Clary removed to Leverett about 1770 and with his two sons, Joseph and Elisha, was conspicuous in the early history of that place. The town records of Leverett contain much concerning this family.

Richard Chauncey removed to Whately and was a founder of the Church which was organized there Aug. 21, 1771.

Josiah Chauncey removed about 1784 to the western part of Albany Co., now Schenectady Co., N. Y., where both himself and his wife are believed to have died within a year from the time of their removal.

Full and well tabulated records of descendants of the early families of Amherst are to be found in the Town Clerk's office at Amherst.

These tables have been carefully compiled from the *History* and *manuscripts* of *Sylvester Judd*, *Olcott's History of Stratford*, *The Strong Family*, *The Tuttle Family*, *Savage's Gen. Dictionary*, *N. E. Hist. and Gen. Register* and other works. If errors should be found they will not invalidate the general conclusions.

ABBREVIATIONS.

b.	born.	d.	died.	m.	married.
B.	Boston.	F.	Farmington.	Sp.	Springfield.
C.	Cambridge.	Hr.	Hartford.	St.	Stratford.
Ch.	Charleston.	L.	Longmeadow.	We.	Wethersfield.
D.	Dedham.	N. H.	New Haven.	Wi.	Windsor.
Dor.	Dorchester.	Reh.	Rehoboth.		

Sons and Daughters.	Amherst Founders.	Third Generation.	Second Generation.	First Settlers.
Martin, b. 1718 Ebenezer.	EBZ. KELLOGG, b. 1695, d. 1766. m. 1716.	NTL KELLOGG. b. 1669, d. 1750. m. 1692.	Jos. Kellogg, F. b. 1628, d. 1708. m. 2nd 1667. Abig. Terry. bap. 1646.	Steph. Terry, Wi. d. 1668
		Sar. Boltwood. b. 1672.	Sam. Boltwood. slain 1704. Sarah Lewis. b. 1652, d. 1722.	Rob. Boltwood, We. d. 1684. Wm. Lewis, Hr. Mary Hopkins.
	ELIZ. INGRAM. b. 1691.	JOHN INGRAM. b. 1661. m. 1689.	John Ingram. b. 1642, d. 1722. m. 1664. Eliz. Gardner. d. 1684.	Sam. Gardner, We. b. 1615, d. 1696.
		MEH. DICKINSON-	Jno Dickinson. d. 1676.	Ntl Dickinson, We. d. 1676. Ntl Foote, We. m. 1646. Eliz. Smith, We. b. 1627. dau. Sam. Smith.
			Frances Foote.	
Sam. '20. Sarah, '25. Philip, '27. John, '30. Reuben. '32. Eben. '37.	John Ingram. b. 1693, d. 1737. m. 1719.	JOHN INGRAM.	See above.	
	LYD. BOLTWOOD. b. 1696, d. 1779.		Sam. Boltwood.	See above.
Elizab. '18. Eben. '20. Sarah '23.	ELEAZ. MATTOON. b. 1690, d. 1767. m. 1715.	Phil. Mattoon. m. 1677. Sarah Hawkes. b. 1657, d. 1751.	Jno. Hawkes, Wi d. 1662.	
	EL. BOLTWOOD. b. 1681.		Sam. Boltwood.	See above.
Jonath. '17. David, '19. Hann'h, '23. John.	JOHN NASH, b. 1694, d. 1778. m. 1716.	John Nash. b. 1667, d. 1743. m. 1691. Eliz. Kellogg. b. 1673, d. 1750.	Timothy Nash. b. 1626, d. 1699. m. 1657. Rebecca Stone. d. 1709. Jos. Kellogg.	Thos. Nash, N. H. Sam. Stone, Hr.
	HAN. INGRAM. b. 1697.	JOHN INGRAM.	See above.	
Son, '25. Jemima '26. Philip, '29. Aaron, '32.	AARON SMITH, b. 1700, d. 1759. m. 1724.	Ichabod Smith. b. 1675, d. 1746. m. 1698.	Philip Smith. b. 1633, d. 1685. Rebecca Foote.	Sam. Smith, We. b. 1602, d. 1680, Ntl Foote, We.
		Eliz. Cook.	Aaron Cook. Sar. Westwood.	Aaron Cook, Wi. Wm. Westwood, Hr.
	MEH. INGRAM, b. 1698.	JOHN INGRAM.	See above.	
Nath., '27, d. 27. Dor'thy. '29. Rebec'a, '31.	NTL SMITH, b. 1702, d. 1789. m. 1726.	Ichabod Smith.	See above.	
	Reb. Ingram. b. 1704.	JOHN INGRAM.	See above.	
Gideon, '20. Ebenezer. Reuben. Joseph, '30. Abigail. Sarah. Mary, '37. Jerusha. Exper. '41.	EBZ. DICKINSON, b. 1696, d. 1780. m. 1720.		Neh. Dickinson. b. 1644, d. 1723. Mary Cowls.	Ntl Dickinson,We. d. 1676. John Cowls, F.
	SAR. KELLOGG. b. 1701, d. 1743.	NTL KELLOGG.	See above.	

Sons and Daughters.	Amherst Founders.	Third Generation.	Second Generation.	First Settlers.
Abigail,'23. Jonath. '28. Martin. David. Noah. '42. Hannah. Rebecca. Jerusha.	JONA. SMITH. b. 1689, d. 1778, m. 1722.	Jona. Smith. d. 1737. m. 1688.	Phil. Smith. b. 1633, d. 1685. Rebec. Foote.	Sam'l Smith, We. Nath'l Foote, We.
		ABIG. KELLOGG. b. 1671.	Jos. Kellogg.	See p. 105.
	HAN'H WRIGHT.	Benoni Wright. b. 1675, d. 1702	Sam'l Wright. slain 1675. m. 1653. Elizabeth Burt.	Sam'l Wright, Sp. Henry Burt, Sp.
		Rebecca Barrett.	Benj. Barrett.	
Elizab., '22. Pelati. '24. Abigail,'26. Lucy. '28.	PELET. SMITH. b. 1694. m. 1721.	Sam'l Smith. b. 1665, d. 1724. m. 1687.	Chileab Smith. b. 1635, d. 1731. m. 1661. Han. Hitchcock. b. 1645, d. 1733.	Sam'l Smith, We. b. 1602, d. 1680. L. Hitchcock, We.
		Sarah Bliss. b. 1697.	Lawr. Bliss. m. 1654. Lydia Wright.	Thos. Bliss, Hr. Sam'l Wright, Sp.
	ABIGAIL WAIT.	Wm. Wait. d. 1732. m. 1681.		
		Sarah Kingsley. b. 1665, d. 1691.	Enos Kingsley. m. 1662. Sarah Haynes.	J. Kingsley, Reh. Edm. Haynes, Sp.
Oliver, '30. Elizab., '32. Eunice, '35. Jerush.,'41. Medad, '44. Abigail,'48.	R. CHAUNCEY. b. 1703, d. 1790. m. 1729.	Is. Chauncey. b. 1670, d. 1745.	Isr.Chauncey,St. b. 1644, d. 1702-3. m. 1667. Mary Nichols.	Ch. Chauncey, C. d. 1671. Catharine Eyre. Isaac Nichols, St.
		Sarah Blackleach. b. 1681, d. 1720.	R.Blackleach,St d. 1731, ae. 78. m. 1680. Abig. Hudson. d. 1712, ae. 60.	John Hudson, N. H.
	ELIZ. SMITH. b. 1708, d. 1790.	Jona. Smith.	See above.	
Elizab., '41. Hannah. Theoda. Mary, '54. Eunice, '56. Naomi. Will'rd, '61.	DAVID SMITH. b. 1707, d. 1771.	Luke Smith. b. 1666. m. 1690.	Chileab Smith.	See above.
		Mary Crow. b. 1672, d. 1761.	Sam'l Crow. slain 1676. m. 1671.	John Crow, Hr. d. 1686. Eliz. Goodwin, Hr. dau. Wm. Goodwin.
			Han'h Lewis.	Wm. Lewis, Hr. Mary Hopkins.
	HAN'H WILLARD. b. 1722, d. 1809.	Josiah Willard. m. 1657.	Simon Willard. b. 1605. Mary Sharpe. b. 1614.	Rich. Willard, C. Henry Sharpe.
		Han'h Hosmer.	Th. Hosmer, Hr.	
Lucy, '46. Dorothy,'48 Jona., '49. Joel, '51. Samuel,'53. Stough.,'55. Daniel, '56.	JONA. DICKINSON. b. 1715. m. 1745.	Sam'l Dickinson. b. 1682, d. 1747. m. 1711.	Neh. Dickinson. Jonathan Marsh. b. 1650, d. 1739. m. 1676. Dorcas.	Ntl Dickinson, We. John Marsh, Hr. d. 1688. Ann Webster. dau. of John, Hr.
		Han'h Marsh. b. 1690.		
		John Stoughton. b. 1683, d. 1746. m. 1706.	John Stoughton. b. 1657, d. 1712. m. 1682. Eliz. Bissell. b. 1666, d. 1688.	Thos. Stoughton. son of Thomas, Wi. Mary Wadsworth. dau. of William, Hr. Thos. Bissell. son of John, Wi. Abigail Moore. dau. of John, Wi.
	DOROTHY STOUGHTON b. 1715.	Eunice Bissell.	Thos. Bissell 2nd b. 1656, d. 1738. m. 1678.	

Sons and Daughters.	Amherst Founders.	Third Generation.	Second Generation.	First Settlers.
Anne. Elijah. Sarah. Zecha, '43. John, '46. Miriam, '49 Mehitabel. Zecha.. '53.	Sam'l Hawley. d. 1750. m. 1736.	SAM'L HAWLEY. b. 1686. m. 1708.	Jos. Hawley.	Th. Hawley, Rox.
			Lyd. Marshall.	S. Marshall, Wi. Mary Wilton, Wi.
		MEH. BELDING. b. 1687.	Sam. Belding. b. 1657, d. 1737. m. 1678.	S. Belding, We. d. 1713.
			Sar. Fellowes. d. 1713.	R. Fellowes, Hr. d. 1683.
	SARAH FIELD. b. 1714.	Zech. Field. b. 1676, d. 1738. m. 1705.	John Field. d. 1717. m. 1670.	Zech. Field, Hr. d. '66.
			Mary Edwards.	A. Edwards, Sp.
		SARAH CLARK.	John Clark. Rebec. Cooper.	Wm. Clark, Dor. Th. Cooper, Wi.
Asena., '39. Joseph, '44. Joseph, '48. Abigail. Rebecca.	Jos. Hawley. d. 1756. m. 1737. REBEC. FIELD. b. 1711.	Sam. Hawley.	See above.	
		Zech. Field.	See above.	
John, '40. Abigail, '42. Martha, '43. Mary, '46. Abigail, '48. Sarah, '50. Eben'r, '52. Samuel, '54. Jemim., '55. Jonath., '59. Zechariah.	John Field. b. 1718.	Zech. Field.	See above.	
	ABIG. BOLTWOOD.	Sam. Boltwood. b. 1679, d. 1738. m. 1703.	Sam. Boltwood.	See p. 105.
		HAN. ALEXANDER.	Ntl Alexander.	G. Alexander, Wi.
			Han'h Allen.	Sam. Allen, Wi. H. Woodford, Hr.
	MAR. BOLTWOOD.	Sam. Boltwood.	See above.	
Mary, '38. Moses.	Moses Warner. b. 1715, d. 1772. m. 1738.	Jacob Warner. b. 1687, d. 1747.	Jacob Warner. d. 1711.	And. Warner, Hr. d. 1684.
			Eliz. Goodman.	R. Goodman, Hr. Mary Terry, Wi.
	Mary Field. b. 1716.	Zech. Field.	See above.	
Ruth, '32. Rhoda, '35. Thom's, '39. Lydia, '42. John, '45. Joseph, '50.	John Morton. m. 1730.	Jos. Morton. b. 1672, d. 1730.	Rich. Morton, Hr. d. 1710.	
		Mary Marsh. b. 1678.	Sam'l Marsh. b. 1645, d. 1728. m. 1667.	John Marsh. Hr. See p. 106.
			Mary Allison.	
	Lydia Hawley. b. 1710, d. 1793.	SAM. HAWLEY.	See above.	
Ephr'm, '42. Martin, '44. Doroth., '46. Abigail, '48. John, '51. Sarah, '53. Joseph, '58.	Eph. Kellogg. b. 1709, d. 1777. m. 1741.	Ntl. Kellogg. b. 1669, d. 1750. m. 1692.	Jos. Kellogg.	See p. 105.
			Abig. Terry.	Step. Terry, Wl.
		Sar. Boltwood. b. 1672.	Sam. Boltwood.	See above.
	Dor. Hawley. b. 1723.	Sam. Hawley.	See above.	

Sons and Daughters.	Amherst Founders.	Third Generation.	Second Generation.	First Settlers.
		Joseph Clary. b. 1677, d. 1748. m. 1702.	John Clary. d. 1688. Ann Dickinson.	John Clary, Wat. N. Dickinson, We.
Sarah, '32. Elisha, '33. Joseph, '36. Joseph, '37. Sarah, '40. Gersh., '42. Gersh., '55.	Joseph Clary. b. 1705. m. 1729.	Han'h Belding. b. 1681.	Sam'l Belding.	See p. 107.
		Sam'l Gunn. b. 1662, d. 1755. m. 1685.	Nth. Gunn, Hr. m. 1658. Sarah Day. slain 1677.	Robt. Day, Hr. E. Stebbins.
	Sarah Gunn. b. 1710.	Eliz. Wyatt. d. 1737.	Jno. Wyatt, Wi. d. 1668. M. Brownson.	J. Brownson, Hr.
Israel, '26. Abia, '29. John, '31. Martha, '34. Mary, '42.	Jno Cowls. b. 1700.	Jona. Cowls. b. 1671, d. 1756. m. 1697.	John Cowls. b. 1641, d. 1711. d. 1668. Debo. Bartlett.	John Cowls, F. d. 1675. Rob't Bartlett, Hr.
	Mary. b. 1706, d. 1795.	Prud. Frary. b. 1677, d. 1756.	Elizar. Frary. d. 1709. m. 1666. Mary Graves. b. 1647.	Jno. Frary, Ded. Isaac Graves, Hr. slain 1677. M. Church, Hr.
Sarah, '32. Oliver, '35. Jerush.,'37. Jonath.,'39. David, '41. Josiah, '44. Eleaz'r, '46. Reuben,'49. Enos, '52. Simeon, '56.	Jona. Cowls. b. 1703, d. 1776. m. 1732.	Jona. Cowls.	See above.	
	Sar. Gaylord. b. 1709, d. 1790.	Sam'l Gaylord. b. 1676, d. 1734. m. 1702.	Wm. Gaylord. b. 1651, d. 1690. m. 1671. Ruth Crow.	Wm. Gaylord, Wi. Ann Porter. John Crow, Hr. d. 1686. Eliz. Goodwin. dau. W. Goodwin, Hr.
		Mary Dickinson.	Neh. Dickinson. b. 1644. Mary Cowls.	Neh. Dickinson, We. Jno. Cowls, F.
	Nathan Moody. b. 1706, d. 1791. m. 1735.	Sam'l Moody. b. 1670, d. 1744. m. 1700.	Sam'l Moody. d. 1689. Sarah Deming. d. 1717.	Jno. Moody, Hr. John Deming, We.
John, '36. Josiah, '40. Abigail,'50. Abigail,'52.		Sarah Lane.	Sam'l Lane. m. 1677. S. Dickinson.	William Lane, B. John Dickinson, We. d. 1676.
	Ab. Montague. b. 1713.	Jno. Montague. b. 1681, d. 1722. m. 1712.	Jno. Montague. d. 1732. m. 1681. Han'h Smith.	R. Montague, We. b. 1614, d. 1681. Abig. Downing. d. 1694. Chileab Smith.
		Mind. Lyman.	Thos. Lyman. m. 1678. Ruth Holten.	Rich. Lyman, Hr. Hep. Ford, Wi. Wm. Holten, Hr. b. 1611, d. 1691.
Elijah, '23. Will'm, '26. Doroth.,' 9. David, '35. Seth, '36. Hann'h,'44.	Wm. Murray. d. 1784. m. 1723. Han'h Dickinson.	Jno. Dickinson. b. 1667, d. 1761. m. 1688. Sarah. d. 1707.	Nth. Dickinson. b. 1643, d. 1710. Hann'h. d. 1679.	N. Dickinson, We.

Sons and Daughters.	Amherst Founders.	Third Generation.	Second Generation.	First Settlers.
		Sam. Wright. b. 1683. m. 1717.	Joseph Wright. b. 1657, d. 1697. m. 1679.	Sam. Wright, Sp. Eliz. Burt, Sp.
	Chas. Wright. b. 1719, d. 1793. m. 1742.		Ruth Sheldon.	Isaac Sheldon, Wl. d. 1708. m. 1653. M. Woodford, Hr.
Solom., '43. Samu'l, '45. Dorcas, '50. Josiah, '52. Sarah, '57. Esther, '60. Solom., '62.		Jemima King.	Sam. King. b. 1664, d. 1701. m. 1690.	John King, Hr. Sarah Holton.
			Johan. Taylor. b. 1665.	John Taylor. slain 1704. m. 1692. Th. Woodward, Dor.
	Ruth Boltwood. b. 1722, d. 1806.	Sol. Boltwood. b. 1694, d. 1762.	Sam. Boltwood.	See p. 105.
		Mary Norton. b. 1686, d. 1763.	John Norton, F. Ruth Moore.	
Cathar.,'41. Doroth.,'44. Isaac, '45.	Ch. Chauncey. b. 1712. m. 1740. Sarah Ingram.	Is. Chauncey.	See p. 106.	
		Ntl. Ingram. b. 1674. m. 1696.	John Ingram.	See p. 105.
Eunice, '48. David, '50.	m. 2nd, 1746.	Esther Smith.	Chil. Smith.	See p. 106.
	Mary Gaylord.	Sam. Gaylord.	See p. 108.	
Eliz.B., '47. Mary. '49. Sarah, '51. Josiah, '53. Isaac, '55. Moses, '57. Moses, '61. Samu'l, '63. Samuel,'64. Josiah, '67.	Josi. Chauncey. b. 1716, d. 1782. Mary.	Is. Chauncey.	See p. ,106	
Nath'el, '28. Wm.II., '30. Rachel, '31. Malachi '32. Jesse, '33. Eber, '34. Timot., '36. Samuel, '37. Ruth, '39. Exper., '39. Mary, '41. David, '44. Jonath.,'17. Benjm., '51.	Ntl. Church. b. 1704. m. 1727.	Sam. Church. b. 1667, d. 1773. m. 1692.	Sam. Church. d. 1684. M. Churchill.	Rich. Church, Hr. d. 1667. J. Churchill.
		Abig. Harrison. b. 1673.	Is. Harrison. M. Montague.	R. Montague, We.
	R. M'Crannery.	W. M'Crannery. m. 1685.		
		Marg. Riley. b. 1692.	John Riley. b. 1646.	John Riley, We.
Stephen, Joel, Titus, Mary, '27.	Stephen Smith. b. 1797, d. 1750.	Jonathan Smith.	See p. 106.	
Moses, '33. Sime'n, '35. Hann'h, '37. Cathar.,'39. Azub'h,'41. Elizab., '43. Amasa, '46. Samuel,'48. Noad'h, '51. Oliver, '55.	Moses Smith. b. 1708, d. 1781. m. 1732.	Ichabod Smith.	See p. 105.	
		Samuel Childs. d. 1756. m. 1709.	Richard Childs.	Rich. Childs, Barkh m. 1649. Mary Linnell, Barkh
			Eliz. Crocker.	John Crocker, Barns m. 1659. Mary Bodfish, Barns
	Hannah Childs.	..	Jos. Barnard. slain 1695.	Francis Barnard, Hr m. 1644. Hannah Marvin, Hr

Sons and Daughters.	Amherst Founders.	Third Generation.	Second Generation.	First Settlers.
			Jos. Parsons. b. 1647, d. 1729. m. 1669.	Jos. Parsons, Hr. d. 1684. m. 1646. Mary Bliss, Hr. b. 1620, d. 1712.
		David Parsons. b. 1680, d. 1743. m. 1707.	Eliz. Strong. b. 1647, d. 1736.	John Strong, Wi. Abig. Ford, Wi.
	DAVID PARSONS. b. 1712, d. 1781. m. 1744.		Thos. Stebbins. b. 1648, d. 1675. m. 1672.	Th. Stebbins, Sp. b. 1620, d. 1683. m. 1645. Han'h Wright, Sp.
		Sarah Stebbins. b. 1686, d. 1759.	Abigail Mun. b. 1650.	Benj. Mun, Hr. m. 1649. Abig. Burt, Sp.
Eunice, '47. David, '49. Eunice, '51. Salome, '53. Mary, '57. Gideon, '59. Gideon, '61. Leon'd, '64.			Rob't Welles. m. 1675.	John Welles, St. b. 1621, d. 1659. m. 1647. Eliz. Bourne, St.
		Gideon Welles. b. 1692, d. 1740. m. 1716.	Eliz. Goodrich. b. 1658, d. 1698.	Wm. Goodrich, Hr. d. 1676. m. 1648. Sarah Marvin, Hr.
	Eunice Welles. b. 1723, d. 1740.		John Chester. b. 1656, d. 1711. m. 1686.	John Chester, Hr. b. 1635, d. 1698. m. 1654. Sarah Welles, Hr.
		Han'h Chester. b. 1696, d. 1749.	Han'h Talcott. b. 1665, d. 1741.	Sam. Talcott, Hr. d. 1691. m. 1654. Han'h Holyoke, Sp. b. 1644, d. 1679.
		Neh. Strong. b. 1694, d. 1772. m. 1728.	Sam. Strong. b. 1652, d. 1732.	John Strong, Wi.
	Simeon Strong. b. 1736, d. 1805. m. 1763.		Esther Clapp.	Edw. Clapp, Dor.
			Jona. French.	John French, Dor.
Simeon, '64. Sally, '66. Hezek., '69. Polly, '75. John, '78. Solom., '80.		Han'h French. b. 1687, d. 1761.	Sarah Warner. b. 1668.	Isaac Warner, Hr. d. 1691. m. 1666. Sar. Boltwood, We.
		Steph. Wright. b. 1690, d. 1763. m. 1707.	Sam. Wright. b. 1654, d. 1734. m. 1678.	Sam. Wright, Sp. m. 1653. Eliz. Burt, Sp.
	Sarah Wright. b. 1739, d. 1783.		Sarah Lyman. b. 1658.	John Lyman, Hr. b. 1623, d. 1690. Dorcas Plum, We.
		Esther Cook. b. 1695.	Noah Cook. b. 1657, d. 1699.	Aaron Cook, Wi. b. 1610, d. 1690. Joan Denslow, Wi. d. 1676.
			Sarah Nash.	Jos. Nash, N. H.
Jona., '49. Jona., '51. Rebecca '54 Nath'l, '56. Lydia, '58. Philip, '60. Sarah, Mary, '66. Hannah Martha, '68.	Jona. Edwards. b. 1712. m. 1748.	N't'l Edwards. Slain 1724. m. 1719.	Sam'l Edwards. slain by Indians	Alex. Edwards, Sp.
		Hannah French b. 1697, d. 1761.	Sarah Pomeroy. See above.	Wi.
		Sam'l Smith. b. 1691, d. 1755-6. m. 2nd, 1724.	Sam'l Smith.	Chileab Smith, We.
	Rebecca Smith.	Sarah Billings. b. 1697.	Sam'l Billings. b. 1665.	Sam'l Billings, Hr. Sarah Fellows, Hr.

Sons and Daughters.	Amherst Founders.	Third Generation.	Second Generation.	First Settlers.
			Sam'l Dickinson. b July 1638.	N'l Dickinson, We.
Nathan, '35 Ebenez.,'41 Irene, '43. Enos, '46.	Nathan Dickinson. b. May 30, 1712. d. Aug. 7, 1796.	Eben. Dickinson. b. Feb. 2, 1681. d. March. 16, 1730. m. June 27, 1706.	d. Nov. 30, 1711. m. Jan. 4, 1668. Marth' Bridgman	Jas. Bridgman, Sp.
		Han'h Frary. b. March 23, 1683.	Eliezer Frary.	See p. 108.
Azar., '52. Elihu, '53. Shelah, '55. Thank'l, '58 Lois, '59. Asa, '61. Levi. Joanna, '66.	Thankful Warner. —— m. 2nd. Joanna Leonard.	Dan'l Warner. b. 1693.	Dan'l Warner. b. 1666, d. 1754. m. 1688. Mary Hubbard. b. 1669.	Dan'l Warner, son of Andrew, Hr. John Hubbard, son of George, We.
—— Stephen, '70 Judith.	—— m. 3rd. Judith Hosmer.			
Lydia, '50. Lucina, '52. Eleazar, '54 Ithamar,'56 Eleazar, '58 Sarah, '60. Ethan, '63. Achsah,'65. Eleazar, '67 Justin, '70. Seth, '75.	Eleazer Smith. b. 1725. d. 1816. Lydia Thomas. . b. 1725. Abigail Hale. b. 1735, d. 1812.	John Smith. b. 1684, d. 1761. m. (?) Esther Colton. b. 1687. Lebanon. Ct. Thomas Hale. b. 1705, d. 1787. m. 1734. Abigail Burt.	John Smith. b. 1661, d. 1727. m. 1683. Joanna Kellogg. b. 1664. Ephraim Colton. b. 1648, d. 1713, m 2nd, 1685. Est. Marshfield. b 1667, d. 1714. Thomas Hale. David Burt.	Phil. Smith, We. Jos. Kellogg, F. Geo. Colton, Sp. Deb. Gardner, Hr. S. Marshfield, Sp. Cath. Chapin, Sp. Thos. Hale, Sp. Prisc. Markham, dau. of William, Hr Nat'l Burt, Sp. Rebécca Sikes, Sp.
Eunice. b. 1750. Simeon, '52. Levi, '53. Judah, '56. Lois, '58. Judah, '59. Asahel, '62. Lois, '64. Justus, '65. Mary, '67. Jerusha,'70 Jerusha,'72	Simeon Clark. b. 1720, d. 1801. m. 1749. Rebecca Strong. b. 1724, d. 1811.	Increase Clark. b. 1684. d. 1775. m. 1710. Mary Sheldon. b. 1690, d. 1767. N't'l Strong. b. 1698, d 1781. m. 1721. Miriam Sheldon. b. 1704, d. 1796.	John Clark. b. 1651, d. 1704. Mary Strong. b. 1654, d. 1738. Isaac Sheldon. b. 1616, d. 1712. m. 1685. Sarah Warner. b. 1667. N't'l Strong. b. 1673. d. 1750. m. 1697. Rebec. Stebbins. b. 1676, d. 1712. Eben. Sheldon. b. 1678, d. 1755. m. 1701. Mary Hunt. b. 1680.	Wm. Clark, Dor. Jno. Strong, Wi. Is. Sheldon Wi. M. Woodford, dau. of Thomas, Hr. Dan'l Warner, Hr. Eben. Strong, Wi. b. 1643, d. 1729, m. 1668. Han'h Clapp. Dor. b. 1646. J. Stebbins, Sp. b. 1626, d 1679. m. 1657. Ab. Bartlett, Hr. d. 1681. Is. Sheldon, Wi. Jona. Hunt, Hr. b. 1637, d. 1691. m. 1662. Cl. Hosmer, Hr.
William,'66 Thank'l, '68 Sarah, '70. Fanny, '72. Seth, '74. Sarah, '77. Eliph.B. '79 Fanny, '81.	Seth Coleman. b. 1740, d. 1816. m. 1765. Sarah Beecher.	N't'l Coleman. b. 1709, d. 1792. m. 1739. Mercy Smith. b. 1715, d. 1798. Eliph. Beecher. b. 1711, d. 1777. m. 1732.	N't'l Coleman. b. 1684, d. 1755. m. 1705. Mary Ely. Chileab Smith. b. 1685, d. 1746. m. 1710. Mercy Golding. Joseph Beecher. b. 1683. m. 1710. Sarah Morris.	J. Coleman, We. b. 1635, d. 1711. m. 1679. Mehit. Root, Hr. Chil. Smith, We. Pet. Golding, B. Jos. Beecher, N. H. b 1645, d. 1712. Jos. Morris, N. H.

B.

PETITION AGAINST BUILDING TWO MEETING HOUSES.

[*Manuscript copied by Rev. J. H. Temple, and deposited in the Library of Amherst College by M. F. Dickinson, Jr.*]

14: 684. Mass. Archives.

To his Excellency Thomas Hutchinson Esq. Captain General and Governor in Chief in and over his Majesty's Province of the Massachusetts Bay in New England and Vice Admiral of the same.

To the Hon[bl] his Majesty's Council and House of Representatives in General Court assembled at Boston on the 26th day of May A. D. 1773.

The subscribing Petitioners Inhabitants of the District of Amherst in the County of Hampshire

Most humbly shew.

That the District of Amherst contains a Tract of Land nearly equal to seven miles in length and three miles in breadth taken together: That in the year 1735, a Precinct or Parish was erected there by the name of the *Third Precinct of Hadley,* in which town said lands then were. That in the year 1738 a Meeting House was erected, and in the year 1739 a Minister was settled there. That in the year 1759 the same Parish or Precinct was erected into a District by the name of Amherst, with some Inhabitants of Hadley Parish with their Farms annexed thereto. That your Petitioners are most of them Inhabitants of the middle Part of the said District, whose Lands and Estates are adjacent to the said Meeting House on each side, and towards each end of the District, and that they and their predecessors were the first original settlers of the Parish of East Hadley, from which said Amherst was erected, who bore the principal part of the burden of beginning and bringing forward the settlement at first, of building a Meeting House, supporting the Ministry and all other charges; and have continued to bear the greater part of Expenses of every kind from the original settlement of the Parish to this day. That though they have long held a state of good agreement and harmony among themselves, and conducted their affairs both ecclesiastical and civil with great unanimity, yet are now in a most unhappy controversy with the inhabitants of the remote parts of the District respecting the building a Meeting House for Public Worship. That partly by reason of the Inhabitants who were admitted from Hadley Parish to be incorporated with Amherst at their own request, and because of their great distance from their own Meeting House, partly by reason of the increase of settlers in the remoter parts and near the two ends of the District, and partly by the methods used by the opposite party to multiply their votes, by transferring property from the father's List to the son's, who tho' qualified according to the letter of the Province Law ought to every equitable purpose to be considered as having no property at all: Your Petitioners, though owning the greater part of the Property within the District, are yet in respect of their number of voters become a minor party, and being as they conceive oppressed and likely still to be oppressed by the strength of a prevailing majority, and being under necessity therefore to seek redress & Protection in Legislative Power, humbly beg leave to open and state their matters of complaint in the following manner (viz.)

That within two years last past the Increase of inhabitants made it needful to provide a new Meeting House for Public Worship: That on a motion for this purpose, the Inhabitants of the remoter settlements towards each end of the District united together in a Design of procuring the District (however small in its extent) to be divided into two Districts, so that the extremities of the two Districts should be at the present Centre, and your Petitioners on each side of the present Meeting House, to be at the remote or extreme parts of the two proposed Districts. This Proposal was brought before a District Meeting holden on the 13th Day of January A. D. 1772, and though opposed by your Petitioners, a vote was then passed for the proposed Division, That from a supposed insufficiency in the proceeding, the same matter was again brought before a District Meeting holden the 10th Day of March in the same year: and there being then an equal number of voters on each side of the question no vote was passed, That afterwards the Party for the Division entered into an agreement for effecting their purpose by procuring a Majority for erecting two Meeting Houses at the joint expense of the whole District before any Division should be made, or any new District erected, and to place them so as to subserve their design of a future Division towards the ends of the present, and in the middle of each proposed District, whereby they apprehended that your Petitioners overpowered by their majority, would be finally brought by compulsion to join with them in procuring such a Division, That pursuant to this design a meeting was holden on the 14th day of April last past, at which (having previously multiplied their voters in the manner above described) they procured a majority for erecting the two Meeting Houses; and a vote was accordingly passed. And tho' nothing as yet hath been done in pursuance of said vote, yet your Petitioners are threatened with the speedy execution of it. All which votes and proceedings, by attested copies thereof herewith exhibited will appear. On which state of facts your petitioners humbly beg leave to represent and observe: That the whole District of Amherst being of no larger extent than nearly as above set forth, cannot admit of having a new District erected therefrom in the manner contended for, without effecting the ruin of the whole, as neither of the two could be able to support public expenses: That the Division contended for is such for which no precedent can be produced, nor any reason assigned: That the very remotest of the Inhabitants have no further travel to the centre of Amherst than what is common to many of the Inhabitants of most of the Towns within the Province. And if any reason could be given for so extraordinary a measure, the same must hold and hold much stronger in almost every Town and District and produce Divisions and subdivisions throughout the whole. That your Petitioners think it most injurious to themselves to be dictated by an opposite Party in respect to their tenderest rights, and especially in matters relating to the Worship of God. That their opponents are unjustly endeavoring to compel them to join in societies wherein they have no disposition to join, and many of them to abandon their Parish, Church and Minister, to which they are most cordially united; and to be so incorporated together in each respective new formed society with those of an adverse Party, of opposite sentiments and exasperated minds: That each of the little, weak and already ruined societies must have nothing in prospect but to be if possible further ruined by increasing Confusion and Discord among themselves. That your Petitioners having acquired their Estates at a rate proportionate to the value of their present situation, may not, consistent with justice, have such privileges wrested from them, That confiding in the Equity of their cause, they would cheerfully have submitted it to the decision of the General Court; but that their opponents (either thro' diffidence of the success of their cause, or for some other reason to your Petitioners unknown) wholly declining to make any application to the General Court for a new District to be erected, have adopted the violent measure of forcing your Petitioners to contribute to the expense of the said two Meeting Houses, which purpose if executed they consider as a manifest oppression under colour of Law, and an high abuse of the Power vested in Towns and Districts by the Acts of this Province. That the vote whereof your Petitioners complain was procured by voters qualified by unfair means, as above expressed, and that your Petitioners having the property of more than half the Estate within the District, and who must therefore bear the greater part of the expense, the whole of which they should esteem to be worse than lost. Your Petitioners further beg leave to represent that during the whole controversy they have adopted every pacific measure; have never used any undue method to multiply their voters, choosing rather to want a majority than to procure it by unfair means, And now finding all attempts of Accommodation to be in vain; and despairing of justice without the intervention of Legislative Power, Your Petitioners most humbly pray the attention of your Excellency and Honors to their unhappy situation. And though they are sensible that no division of Amherst can be made without great prejudice to the whole, and if left to their own election should be very far from desiring it in any manner whatever; Yet since the opposite Party seem resolved to please their own humor at the expense of your Petitioners' ruin, Your Petitioners most humbly pray your Excellency and Honors to interpose for their relief, by allowing them, whose interests and sentiments are united, to be a corporation and Parish by themselves in the middle of Amherst, enjoying all privileges, and being liable to all duties of a Parochial nature that are incumbent on the District of Amherst, leaving our Opponents their election to remain with us on reasonable terms; or be incorporated together among themselves as their remote situation will best permit, or join to be incorporated with some adjacent towns or Parishes, as they can obtain consent for admittance there. And if the granting your Petitioners prayer herein, should seem to throw their opponents into much calamity, which your petitioners by no means desire, if it may be avoided; Yet since our opponents which are now the Major Party will be content with nothing short of *Division* and *Division* to be effected by such violent means, your Petitioners humbly pray your Excellency and Honors to make such a Division as will save and protect *an injured and innocent Party:* and suffer our opponents rather to be ruined alone, than leave them the Power of involving your Petitioners with them: Otherwise that your Excellency and Honors would provide for our safety by passing an Act or Order for depriving the District of Amherst of the power of raising or assessing any monies on the Inhabitants for the building of such Meeting Houses, or for excusing y'r petitioners from contributing any proportion of any Taxes raised for such purpose; or grant relief to your Petitioners in any other way or manner as you in y'r great wisdom shall think fit. And for the preventing any contention or disturbances that might arise in the District between the Parties in the mean time, y'r Petitioners most humbly pray that an Order may be passed for staying all proceedings, either in erecting said Meeting Houses, or in Demolishing the present Meeting House until the final Determination of y'r Excellency & Honors hereon. They also pray that a committee of the General Court may be appointed to repair to Amherst, to examine into the Matters alledged in this Petition if y'r Excellency & Honors think fit: And that all the costs arising by this application may be ordered to be paid by the District of Amherst.

And as in duty bound shall pray

Josiah Chauncey	John Morton	Noah Dickinson
Simeon Strong	Moses Cook	Simeon Pomeroy
Jona Dickinson	Jona Dickinson Jr.	Joseph Dickinson
Jonathan Cowls	David Blodgett	David Hawley
John Field	Gid Dickinson Jr.	Thomas Bascom
Nathan Moody	Reuben Cowls	Eph'm Kellogg Jr.
Alex'r Smith	John Billings	Jonathan Smith
Moses Warner	Thomas Hastings	Jona Nash Jr.
Daniel Kellogg	Samuel Gould	Martin Smith
Elisha Ingram	Moses Warner	Joel Billings
Nathan Dickinson	David Smith	Thomas Hastings Jr.
Hezekiah Belding	Simeon Clark	Nathaniel Smith
W'm Boltwood	Joseph Bolles	Gideon Dickinson
Jona Edwards	Hezekiah Howard	Barnabas Sabin
Nathaniel Coleman	Timothy Clap	Edward Elmer
Jonathan Moody	Simeon Peck	John Morton Jr.
Gideon Henderson	Eben'r Kellogg	David Stockbridge
Nath'l Alex'r Smith	Aaron Warner	Josiah Moody
Jonathan Nash	John Field Jr.	Eben'r Dickinson
Isaac Goodale	Noah Smith	Seth Coleman
Elijah Baker	Joseph Church	John Nash
Solo'm Boltwood	Noadiah Lewis	Joseph Morton
Waitstill Hastings	Silas Matthews	
Nath'l Peck	Timothy Hubbard	

I do hereby certify that the whole Rateable Estate of Amherst as footed by the Assessors on their last List amounts to £7800 : 0

And of that sum what belongs to one of the Anabaptist persuasion, and others not Inhabitants of Amherst amounts to £202 : 15

And that the Estate of the above named Petitioners on the List amounts to £4220 : 13

Seth Coleman
District Clerk.

At a meeting of the District Jan. 26, 1774 it was "Voted to Choose two Agents to Refer a Petition to the General Court to obtain the Division of the District," also "to Authorise two Men to Make answer to the general Court's Citation in Consequence of a Petition of a Number of Inhabitants of Amherst." Choice was made of Reuben Dickinson and Moses Dickinson to fill both positions.

After the hearing the General Court ordered that a committee consisting of Artemas Ward Esq. of the Council and Mr. Pickering and Col. Bacon of the House "repair to the District of Amherst, view the same, hear the parties on the spot, and make report what they think proper for the Court to do thereon: and that the Inhabitants of s^d District in the mean time wholly surcease & forbear all proceedings relative to the building any new Meeting House or Houses in said District."

Pending further action, there came the agitation over the oppressions of the Crown, and then the Revolution. It is interesting to observe that the very meeting in Amherst which sent the "two Agents" to Boston to appear before the General Court in behalf of dividing the District also chose "a Com'tee of Corrispondence to Refer with the Com'tee of Corrispondence in the town of Boston," and that the same Reuben Dickinson and Moses Dickinson were put on this committee with three others none of whom were of the petitioners.

Plainly the way was open for them to unite with the revolutionary party and all the circumstances conspired to promote the union. So, too, it became natural for the petitioners to fall into the opposing conservative party.

Until this time Josiah Chauncey and Simeon Strong had been more prominent in official positions than any others in the place. They had been Justices of the Peace,—the former since 1758 and the latter since 1768; they had been Moderators of the District Meetings, too, and had served often on important committees. But now there is a complete change. Moses Dickinson is made Justice of the Peace, and he and Reuben Dickinson appear continually in the most important stations, while Chauncey and Strong are passed by.

An explanation of this may be found in the petition. The first subscriber to it was Josiah Chauncey and the second Simeon Strong. There can be no doubt that they were the principal authors of it and that their masterly leadership thwarted the scheme of the carefully consolidated majority and prevented the division of the town.

G.

THE ORIGIN OF THE SECOND CHURCH AND PARISH.

The following official document furnished by Mr. J. W. Allen, Clerk of the Second Parish, gives the names of those who were identified with that Parish at its origin.

IN THE YEAR OF OUR LORD 1783.
AMHERST INCORPORATED.
CHAP. III.

An Act for incorporating a Number of the Inhabitants of the Town of *Amherst* in the County of *Hampshire*, into a separate Parish, by the Name of the Second Parish in the Town of *Amherst*

Whereas a number of the inhabitants of the town of *Amherst*, in the said county, herein-after named, have petitioned this Court to be incorporated into a separate parish, for reasons set forth in the petition

Therefore be it enacted by the Senate and House of Representatives in General Court assembled and by the authority of the same. That the said petitioners, namely.

Nathan Dickinson	Moses Dickinson.	John Billing.
John Dickinson.	Joseph Eastman.	Ebenezer Mattoon.
Timothy Green.	Pelatiah Smith	*Ebenezer Dickinson,*
Noah Dickinson,	*Hezekiah Belding*	Ebenezer Williams.
Henry Franklin.	John Robins	Jacob Warner.
Abijah Williams.	Joseph Robins.	James Merrick second,
Azariah Dickinson,	John Ingraham	Andrew Kimbal
Samuel Henry,	Nathan Perkins.	*Noadiah Lewis.*
Noah Hawley.	Ebenezer Dickinson third	*Joseph Morton.*
Oliver Clapp.	Lemuel Moody	Giles Church.
Ebenezer Eastman	Nathan Dickinson junior,	Nathaniel Dickinson 2d.
Gideon Moore,	Stephen Cole.	Waitstill Dickinson.
Thomas Marshall.	Amariah Dana.	John Eastman,
Joseph Dickinson.	David Cowls,	David Rich,
Simeon Cowls,	Benanuel Leach.	Elihu Dickinson,
Abner Adams,	Joseph Eastman junior,	Reuben Ingraham,
Samuel Ingraham,	Reuben Dickinson,	Clement Marshall,
Thomas Morton.	Reuben Dickinson junior,	Ebenezer Dickinson 2d,
Ebenezer Mattoon junior,	Amos Ayres,	Aaron Billing,
Justus Williams,	Adam Rice.	Gideon Lee,
Jacob Warner, junior,	Solomon Dickinson,	Levi Dickinson,
Asa Dickinson,	Ebenezer Ingraham,	Nathan Perkins junior,
Eli Putnam,	Zimri Dickinson.	Joseph Williams,
David Blodget junior,	Phineas Allen,	Simeon Dickinson,

and Gad Dickinson together with their estates which they now have, or may hereafter possess, in their own right, in the said town of *Amherst*, be, and hereby are incorporated into a separate parish by the name of the second parish in the town of *Amherst*.

Comparing these names with those on page 115 it will be found that eight appear in both lists. These are Italicised above. One other name of the former list, that of *Gideon Henderson*, is found on the earliest roll of members of the Second Church. Of these nine men, seven had served on the Committees of Correspondence and four had been in the army.

During the Revolution there had been eight Committees of Correspondence with twenty-nine different members. Nineteen of these are named in the above list. There are twenty-four names of this list which are to be found in the rolls of soldiers published by Rev. P. W. Lyman. In these rolls about one hundred and fifty soldiers in all are accredited to Amherst.

Several prominent officers were in this movement to form the Second Parish. Capt. Reuben Dickinson, Capt. Ebenezer Mattoon, Lieut. Noah Dickinson and Lieut. Joseph Dickinson. Capt. Mattoon was especially conspicuous; the meetings of the Councils were at his house, and the final Council was popularly spoken of as Capt. Mattoon's Council.*

On the side of the Old Church Josiah Chauncey and Simeon Strong are conspicuous leaders again. The Committee for the Ordination of Mr. Parsons consisted of these two with Seth Coleman: the Committee " to treat with the aggrieved Brethren," a little later, of them with Dea. Eleazar Smith: and the Committee to make a statement of the case of the Church before the subsequent Council, of them with Dea. Jonathan Edwards.

The Council called for the Ordination of Mr. Parsons was as follows:

> The First Church in Springfield Rev. Robert Breck
> The Church in Sunderland Rev. Joseph Ashley
> " " " Northfield Rev. John Hubbard
> " " " Hadley Rev. Sam'l Hopkins
> " " " Greenfield Rev. Roger Newton
> " " " Barre Rev. Josiah Dana
> " " " Granby Rev. Simon Backus

---
*An examination of state papers by Mr. John Jameson of Boston confirms the view that this withdrawal from the old Church was mainly for political reasons.

Below are extracts from the Diary of Rev. Enoch Hale of Westhampton, copied by Rev. George Lyman from the original manuscripts now in the possession of Rev. Dr. E. E. Hale of Boston.

"Sep. 30. 1782 Ride to Amherst to Ebenezer Mattoon's to join in Council to advise the aggrieved party.

<table>
<tr><td>Rev. Elders</td><td>Delegates</td></tr>
<tr><td>Jona. Judd. Moderator</td><td>Dea. King. S. Hamp.</td></tr>
<tr><td>Joseph Strong. Scribe.</td><td>———— Williamsburg</td></tr>
<tr><td>Rufus Wells.</td><td>Dea. Salmon White. Whateley</td></tr>
<tr><td>Jos. Lyman.</td><td>Dea. Elijah Morton, Hatfield</td></tr>
<tr><td>Sol. Williams,</td><td>Ephm Wright Esq., N. Hamp.</td></tr>
<tr><td>Enoch Hale,</td><td>Dea. Reuben Wright, W. Hamp.</td></tr>
</table>

Oct 1st Hear and consult.

" 2 Attend ordination of Mr. Parsons, Rev. Breck preached: Hopkins gave charge: Dana prayed first: Hubbard of Northfield prayed to ordain: Morton prayed last: Backus gave right hand.

Return to Council. hear and consult till 12 or 1 o'clock.

Oct. 3. Result and dissolve.

Oct. 28. To Amherst again in Council. Mr. Sylvester Judd. delegate

Nov. 11. To Amherst on Council. to Capt. Mattoon's, by adjournment—hear parties.

Nov. 12, Aggrieved party make proposal to offer Mr. Parsons and his church in answer to theirs made them last even. which I drew for the Committee and which the Council approves, but judge the offer made by the other party unequal and insufficient. Advise the party if their proposal of uniting in the choice of a Mutual Council is not complied with in four weeks to proceed to organize and settle a minister."

The account in the Records of the First Church is as follows:

" Many of the members of the chh, left the worship and communion of the church and formed themselves in a distinct society by agreeing among themselves.

They sent to the church a paper called the Testimony and Representation signed by twenty one members of ye church purporting their dissatisfaction. . . . These aggrieved, as they styled themselves, presented the church with a report of an ex parte council dated Oct. 28, '82 . . which was read at a meeting Nov. 10th and the following votes passed.

Whether this church will appear before an Ecclesiastical Council. chosen by a number of the Bréthren who style themselves the aggrieved. at their adjournment? Voted in the negative. Upon a second question Whether this church will unite with the aggrieved Brethren in the choice of a mutual council and submit to their decision the matter referred to in the Testimony and Representation? Voted in the affirmative.

Voted, To send the aggrieved committee a letter offering to unite with them in ye choice of a mutual council—signed by ye pastor."

At a meeting Nov. 24th. " Voted, That Simeon Strong Esq. Josiah Chauncey Esq., and Dea, Eleazar Smith be a Com'tee to treat with the aggrieved upon the subject of submitting all matter of grievance to a Mutual Council. Voted That they present the aggrieved with a letter of Proposals of Submission."

At a meeting Dec. 3rd. "The Com'tee appointed to treat with the aggrieved Brethren presented the church with a letter purporting the aggrieved would not agree to the church's proposals of Submission to a Mutual Council. Voted That this church will invite an Ecclesiastical Council to look into the affairs of the church and give their advice respecting the Brethren who style themselves aggrieved."

Fifteen churches were invited to this council, but only seven were represented. Those printed in Italics constituted the council.

The Church in Northfield, Rev John Hubbard. Seth Field Esq.
" " " *Greenfield. Rev. Roger Newton. Dea. E. Graves*
" " " Hadley, Rev. Sam'l Hopkins
" " " Granby, Rev. Simon Backus
" *First Church in Springfield, Rev. Robt Breck, Mr. Robt Church*
The Church in W. Springfield, Rev. Jos. Lathrop
" " " Suffield, Rev. Ebenezer Gay.
" " " East Windsor. Rev. Thos. Potwine
" " " *W. Windsor, N. Parish, Rev Theo. Hinsdale, Capt. Nathan Hayden.*
" " " Hartford, Rev. Nathan Strong.
" " " *Barre, Rev Josiah Dana, Mr. Nathan Jennison.*
" " " Rutland. Rev. Jos. Buckminster
" " " Spencer, Rev. Joseph Pope.
" " " *Brookfield, E. Parish, Rev. Nathan Fiske, Capt. Seth Bannister*
" " " *Belchertown, Rev. Justus Forward, Dea Edward Smith*

According to present usage a council composed of a minority of the churches invited would not be competent to transact business.

In this case, however, the council prepared a result, and at a meeting of the church Jan. 19, 1783 it was voted to accept the same. It recommended the church to "exercise forbearance and condescension towards their Brethren who had unwarrantably withdrawn from their communion and cordially to receive them upon their return, deeming their return a sufficient retraction of their errors."

It is not clear wherein lay the particular difficulty that prevented the calling of a mutual council when both parties seem to have strongly desired it. Remembering, however, that on one side were several old army officers and that they had for counsellors a number of ministers who had been ardent advocates of the Revolution (among them a brother of Nathan Hale the martyr) and that on the other side were men who had disbelieved in the Revolution from the start, it may not seem strange that they found causes of disagreement on the subject at issue.

Had a mutual council been called it might, perhaps, have healed the bitter and painful division.

From our point of view it would seem that both of the councils, that of "the aggrieved" and that of the old Church, made a great mistake in not refusing to give other advice than that a competent mutual council be called. Nothing can be plainer now than the inability of either of these councils, as they were constituted, to deal effectively with the case in hand and to accomplish what needed to be done. In the perspective of a century, however, the aspect of things is wholly changed.

NOTE. On page 100, tenth line from the bottom, read, " on *part* of the same Lot."
On page 104 add to Abbreviations, *Barkh.* for Barkhamstead; *Barns.* for Barnstable; *Rox.* for Roxbury; *Wat.* for Watertown.

STATISTICS OF THE CHURCH.
TABULATED CHIEFLY FROM ANNUAL REPORTS TO THE GENERAL ASSOCIATION.

For Year Ending Jan. 1.	Members.				Admitted.			Removed.				Bapt.		Sab. School.
	Males.	Females.	Total.	Absent.	Prof.	Letter.	Total.	De.	Dis.	Ex.	Tot.	Adult.	Infant.	
1828	47	113	160		37	3	40	1	3			13	29	
1829					9	6	15							
1830					3	6	9							
1831					1	8	9							
1832			173		93	7	100	6	4			24	15	
1833					7	2	9							
1834	84	143	227		2	7	9	1	4			1	5	260
1835					6	25	28							
1836			205		1	4	5	1	11	1	13			
1837	65	133	198		3	6	9	1	15	1				248
1838	67	128	195		7	15	22	5	20		25	3	14	300
1839	89	183	272		63	36	99	6	16		22	18	34	300
1840					4	11	15							
1841					4	11	15							
1842	90	180	270		4	16	20	7	15		23	2	16	
1843	92	185	277		15	12	27	9	9	1	19		9	250
1844	96	192	288		9	10	19	3	11		14			
1845	92	187	279		7	4	11	5	15		20		13	300
1846	105	221	326		52	10	62	3	12		15	10	30	250
1847	103	222	325		7	5	12	6	7		13		8	200
1848	96	213	309		2		2	3	15		18		12	160
1849	95	205	300		1	5	6	3	12		15		9	200
1850	86	195	281			3	3	9	12	1	22		9	200
1851	122	235	357		86	9	95	4	15		19	24	7	200
1852	121	229	350		11	4	15	5	2		7		8	
1853			336		2	6	8							
1854	116	231	347			19	19	4	4		8		8	140
1855	113	227	340	42	2	10	12	6	13		19		11	150
1856	114	222	336	64	13	6	19	8	4		12	3	2	150
1857	110	212	322	57	1	12	13	8	16		24		7	226
1858	105	227	332	60	7	17	24	8	11		19		6	200
1859	112	234	346	45	25	7	32	1	14		15	8	4	200
1860	89	212	301	27	9	10	19	6	23	27	56	4	3	210
1861	86	220	306	39	2	12	14	5	3		8	1	3	208
1862	83	211	294	32	2	1	3	4	11		15		6	246
1863	77	212	289	33	1	3	4	5	4		9		4	273
1864	90	214	304	42	1	11	12	6	3		9		5	281
1865	88	239	327	42	31	12	43	6	12		18	7	6	175
1866	84	233	317	42	2	4	6	4	11	1	16		6	170
1867	84	225	309			4	4	2	9		11	6	3	226
1868	91	244	335	17	14	19	33	4	3		7	7	2	255
1869	80	242	322	36	4	16	20	4	10		14	2	3	250
1870	103	271	374	43	29	39	68	10	12		22	9	7	302
1871	108	278	386	51	6	21	27	10	5		15		8	279
1872	112	277	389	55	2	7	9	8	6		14		6	225
1873	104	282	386	55	7	21	28	9	8		17	3	3	240
1874	123	292	415	44	28	14	42	4	17		21	11	4	280
1875	124	278	402	35	13	1	14	10	11		21	1	6	336
1876	125	281	406	30	1	25	26	7	15		22		1	375
1877	123	278	401	69	1	12	13	9	7	1	17			275
1878	113	260	373	70		3	3	4	16		20		1	235
1879	123	295	418	43	51	24	75	9	24		33			310
1880	128	294	422	47	7	25	32	10	12	6	28			300
1881	134	306	440	65	7	25	32	5	5	2	12	2	6	342
1882	130	314	444	67	7	26	33	6	24		30	2	1	325
1883	140	332	472	77	38	19	57	8	21		29	16	1	294
1884	121	306	427	53		13	13	15	33		48		2	276
1885	120	315	435	54	19	24	43	7	28		35	2	3	333
1886	120	320	440	52	15	9	24	2	16	1	19	4	2	350
1887	125	322	447	66	13	17	30	7	16		23	6	3	316
1888	128	325	453	65	16	16	32	10	16		26	7	1	330
1889	130	337	467	74	36	10	46	13	19		32	21	2	309
1890	127	318	445	58	4	9	13	7	24	4	35	3	4	306

BENEVOLENT CONTRIBUTIONS.

The method of preparing these reports has varied from year to year. In some years they are fuller than in others, but necessarily they are incomplete always.

FOR YEAR ENDING JAN'Y 1.	FOREIGN MISSIONS.	EDUCA-TION.	CHURCH BUILDING.	HOME MISSIONS.	AM. MIS. ASSOC.	PUBLICA-TION.	OTHERS.	TOTAL.
1866								1,020
1867								864
1868								1,490
1869								829
1870	595		78	238	102	97	66	1,176
1871								1,025
1872	284			103	51		1,476	1,914
1873	415		40	59	110		156	780
1874								1,137
1875	278	10	18	165		31	357	859
1876	265	10	30	117	36		165	623
1877	484		75	170	32		180	941
1878	514			82	20			616
1879	755		37	613	140	76	700	2,321
1880	597		20	335	86	54	290	1,382
1881	305		31	603	100	77	312	1,428
1882	407		33	413	199	20	110	1,182
1883	563	113	25	301	150	59	610	1,821
1884	464	46	8	297	90	43	200	1,148
1885	633			418	130	155	555	1,891
1886	545	60	12	658	130	60	188	1,653
1887	705	57	16	1,033	233	43	143	2,230
1888	843	118	25	775	164	12	59	1,996
1889	1,008	190	12	594	195	10	362	2,371
1890	701	692	18	792	261	45	117	2,626

www.ingramcontent.com/pod-product-compliance
Lightning Source LLC
Chambersburg PA
CBHW022135160426
43197CB00009B/1302